Contents

Cambridge Certificate in Advanced English 4

WITH ANSWERS

Official examination papers from University of Cambridge ESOL Examinations

CAMBRIDGE
UNIVERSITY PRESS

CAMBRIDGE UNIVERSITY PRESS
Cambridge, New York, Melbourne, Madrid, Cape Town, Singapore,
São Paulo, Delhi, Dubai, Tokyo, Mexico City

Cambridge University Press
The Edinburgh Building, Cambridge CB2 8RU, UK

www.cambridge.org
Information on this title: www.cambridge.org/9780521156905

First published 2010

Printed in the United Kingdom at the University Press, Cambridge

A catalogue record for this publication is available from the British Library

ISBN 978-0-521-156899 Student's Book without answers
ISBN 978-0-521-156905 Student's Book with answers
ISBN 978-0-521-156912 Audio CD Set
ISBN 978-0-521-156929 Self-study Pack

Introduction

This collection of four complete practice tests comprises papers from the University of Cambridge ESOL Examinations Certificate in Advanced English (CAE) examination; students can practise these tests on their own or with the help of a teacher.

The CAE examination is part of a suite of general English examinations produced by Cambridge ESOL. This suite consists of five examinations that have similar characteristics but are designed for different levels of English language ability. Within the five levels, CAE is at Level C1 in the Council of Europe's *Common European Framework of Reference for Languages: Learning, teaching, assessment*. It has also been accredited by the Qualifications and Curriculum Authority in the UK as a Level 2 ESOL certificate in the National Qualifications Framework. The CAE examination is widely recognised in commerce and industry and in individual university faculties and other educational institutions.

Examination	Council of Europe Framework Level	UK National Qualifications Framework Level
CPE Certificate of Proficiency in English	C2	3
CAE Certificate in Advanced English	C1	2
FCE First Certificate in English	B2	1
PET Preliminary English Test	B1	Entry 3
KET Key English Test	A2	Entry 2

Further information

The information contained in this practice book is designed to be an overview of the exam. For a full description of all of the above exams, including information about task types, testing focus and preparation, please see the relevant handbooks which can be obtained from Cambridge ESOL at the address below or from the website at: www.CambridgeESOL.org

University of Cambridge ESOL Examinations
1 Hills Road
Cambridge CB1 2EU
United Kingdom

Telephone: +44 1223 553997
Fax: +44 1223 553621
e-mail: ESOLHelpdesk@ucles.org.uk

The structure of CAE: an overview

The CAE examination consists of five papers.

Paper 1   Reading   1 hour 15 minutes
This paper consists of **four** parts, each containing one text or several shorter pieces. There are 34 questions in total, including multiple choice, gapped text and multiple matching.

Paper 2   Writing   1 hour 30 minutes
This paper consists of **two** parts which carry equal marks. In Part 1, which is **compulsory**, input material of up to 150 words is provided on which candidates have to base their answers. Candidates have to write either an article, a letter, a proposal, or a report of between 180 and 220 words.

In Part 2, there are four tasks from which candidates **choose one** to write about. The range of tasks from which questions may be drawn includes an article, a competition entry, a contribution to a longer piece, an essay, an information sheet, a letter, a proposal, a report and a review. The last question is based on the set books. These books remain on the list for two years. Look on the website, or contact the Cambridge ESOL Local Secretary in your area for the up-to-date list of set books. The question on the set books has two options from which candidates **choose one** to write about. In this part, candidates have to write between 220 and 260 words.

Paper 3   Use of English   1 hour
This paper consists of **five** parts and tests control of English grammar and vocabulary. There are 50 questions in total. The tasks include gap-filling exercises, word formation, lexical appropriacy and sentence transformation.

Paper 4   Listening   40 minutes (approximately)
This paper consists of **four** parts. Each part contains a recorded text or texts and some questions including multiple choice, sentence completion and multiple matching. There is a total of 30 questions. Each text is heard twice.

Paper 5   Speaking   15 minutes
This paper consists of **four** parts. The standard test format is two candidates and two examiners. One examiner takes part in the conversation while the other examiner listens. Both examiners give marks. Candidates will be given photographs and other visual and written material to look at and talk about. Sometimes candidates will talk with the other candidates, sometimes with the examiner and sometimes with both.

Grading

The overall CAE grade is based on the total score gained in all five papers. Each paper is weighted to 40 marks. Therefore, the five CAE papers total 200 marks, after weighting. It is not necessary to achieve a satisfactory level in all five papers in order to pass the examination. Certificates are given to candidates who pass the examination with grade A, B or C. A is the highest. D and E are failing grades. All candidates are sent a Statement of Results which includes a graphical profile of their performance in each paper and shows their relative performance in each one.

For further information on grading and results, go to the website (see page 5).

Test 1

PAPER 1   READING (1 hour 15 minutes)

Part 1

You are going to read three extracts which are all concerned in some way with fashion. For questions **1–6**, choose the answer (**A, B, C** or **D**) which you think fits best according to the text. Mark your answers **on the separate answer sheet.**

What I wear to work
Gayle Mellor (31), Modern Languages teacher

We don't have a dress code as such. The male teachers wear ties, but there is a really diverse approach to smart style amongst the female staff. Respect comes from body language and behaviour rather than the clothes you wear, but of course certain things would be deemed inappropriate, and I've got no problem with that. It's not my choice of outfit that puts me in the mood for work, because I wear my work clothes socially as well, but when I pick up my big satchel, I can feel myself going into 'teacher mode' because it's got all my stuff in it.

What you wear as a teacher does impact on your relationship with the pupils though, especially the girls. If we wear jeans on non-teaching days, the younger ones giggle about it, which is harmless enough. Then you occasionally eavesdrop on the older girls doing a hard-hitting TV-style commentary on what the staff are wearing, which can be unnerving. But the popular stereotype of teachers wearing hard-wearing materials like corduroy only makes me laugh, because I love it! Sometimes, if older pupils like something you wear, they'll ask where it's from, which can contribute to breaking down barriers. If you asked my colleagues, they'd say sky blue skirts have become a bit of a signature for me. Not that I mind, because my wardrobe is built around styles and colours that I feel most comfortable in, and I wouldn't change that.

1   What point does Gayle make about the clothes she wears for teaching?

    A   They should put her in the right frame of mind for work.
    B   She needs to dress smartly if she is to keep her pupils' respect.
    C   Following fashion helps her to understand her pupils' attitudes better.
    D   There are limits to the range of clothes that she considers suitable.

2   Gayle sometimes feels slightly uncomfortable when

    A   people can tell she is a teacher from her clothes.
    B   younger pupils find her clothes amusing.
    C   pupils criticise their teachers' clothes.
    D   people associate her with one particular style of clothes.

Extract from a novel

Mrs Mintar

As Mrs Mintar turned to face him, Inspector Thanet saw her properly for the first time. She was, he realised, well into her seventies. He had been misled by her slim, wiry figure, the vigour with which she moved, and her hair, which was a deep chestnut brown without a trace of grey and was cut in a cropped modern style. She was wearing cinnamon-coloured linen trousers and a loose long-sleeved silk tunic in the same colour. Around her neck was a leather thong from which an intricately carved wooden pendant was suspended. The effect was stylish, somewhat unconventional, and not exactly what Thanet would have expected of

line 9 Ralph Mintar's mother. What would he have expected if he'd thought about it? What was it his wife called that flowery print material? Liberty Lawn, that was it. Yes, made up into a dress with a high neck and full skirt. No, Mrs Mintar senior definitely wasn't the Liberty Lawn type.

She sighed: 'Oh, I suppose I'm the one who'll have to give you all the dreary details, as there's no one else here.' She turned to peer out of the window again. 'Where on earth has Ralph got to? He surely should be back by now.'

'Won't you sit down, Mrs Mintar,' said Thanet. 'I need as much information as you can give me.'

3 In this passage, we learn that Inspector Thanet had previously

   A made a wrong assumption about Mrs Mintar's knowledge of the case.
   B formed a wrong impression of Mrs Mintar's likely age.
   C been misled about Mrs Mintar's willingness to talk to him.
   D been misinformed about how Mrs Mintar looked.

4 What does 'it' in line 9 refer to?

   A a type of fabric
   B an item of jewellery
   C Mrs Mintar's attitude to her son
   D Mrs Mintar's taste in clothes

THE POLO SHIRT

In clothing terms it is the great leveller; neither scruffy nor stuffy, worn sloppily with jeans or neatly under tailored clothes, it never seems out of place. As Christophe Lemaire of fashion label Lacoste explains: 'Sportswear has been the main style revolution of the past fifty years and, after jeans, the polo shirt is its biggest icon.' And yet anybody can wear a polo shirt. Although it has certainly had its fashion highs and lows, essentially the man in the street will wear it any time.

Certainly at polo matches, the polo shirt transcends any kind of issues of fashion.

But more than any other item of clothing that has ever migrated from specialist sportswear to everyday wear – more than football shirts or baseball caps – the polo shirt has cut its ties with its roots and now stands alone. For many, the polo shirt suggests youth rebellion before it recalls sporting greats. Fred Perry was a champion tennis player, but the British brand that takes his name has seen its polo shirt rooted in pivotal style movements associated with youth culture from the 1960s to the present day.

5   In the first paragraph the writer is keen to stress

A   how versatile the polo shirt has proved to be.
B   how consistently fashionable the polo shirt has been.
C   how the polo shirt has lost some of its original appeal.
D   how the polo shirt has influenced trends in sportswear.

6   What is suggested about the polo shirt in the second paragraph?

A   It has increased the fashionable appeal of polo.
B   It is no longer connected to polo in people's minds.
C   It has changed in ways that now make it unsuitable for polo.
D   Its links with youth culture have made it less popular amongst polo players.

Part 2

You are going to read an extract from a newspaper article. Six paragraphs have been removed from the extract. Choose from the paragraphs **A–G** the one which fits each gap (**7–12**). There is one extra paragraph which you do not need to use. Mark your answers **on the separate answer sheet.**

The Modern Adventurer

A real adventure is hard to find these days, says Ed Douglas. It seems that the only things left to explore are marketing opportunities.

I have never met Kevin Foster and know virtually nothing about him, but he has my admiration. Not because he's visited the summit of the highest mountain in each of the fifty states in the US bar one. Not even because he did it on a bicycle.

7	

Such candour is rare in the increasingly narcissistic world of the modern adventurer. In a desperate need to find new 'firsts' to tempt sponsors to part with their cash, the idea of what constitutes a worthwhile achievement has been stretched beyond reason.

8	

Paying for it, on the other hand, is a mountain in itself. That's why the folk who do these things spend more time thinking about marketing strategies and making their websites attractive than they do thinking about tundra and icebergs. An ascent of Everest can cost up to US$70,000; a trip to Antarctica even more. So it's not surprising that they needed to find some new angle to tempt sponsors into handing over the dough.

9	

The adventurer's grand slam, as he termed it, involved climbing the highest mountain on each of the seven continents, taking in both Poles, North and South, on the way. Children the world over had the chance to watch his progress on television or the internet, while he criticised other famous adventurers for being 'too professional'. Climbing those summits, first done in 1986 by Texan oil magnate Dick Bass, is now considered no great challenge by itself. Most of the peaks involve little more than a stiff walk. But few people understand that, least of all the television people who allow the self-publicists seemingly endless airtime in which to promote their sponsors.

Apart from the micro-distinctions, there are other tricks the adventurers use to get our attention. For decades, explorers have been reliving the journeys of the past in a sort of adventure heritage experience, and now we even have re-creations of re-creations.

10	

Then there are those who go on adventures to raise money for charity, people who, unlike Kevin Foster, don't accept the idea that what they are doing is ridiculous. These heroes raise money for good causes to give their exotic holiday moral legitimacy. Some people walk across South America for children's charities, others without nearby mountains to climb settle for abseiling off the highest building in their town for the local hospital's scanner appeal.

11

With a similar commitment to environmental causes, there is a growing band of adventurers who have a genuine concern for the future of the planet. Scores of do-gooders, for example, have trudged up to the foot of Everest, intent on clearing the mountain of the tons of garbage left behind by previous expeditions.

12

In the same way, the sight of a minor celebrity climbing aboard a hot-air balloon for another abbreviated flight does make a welcome change from reading about all the usual unpleasant wars and disasters. And I, for one, plan to become part of this new wave of optimism. As far as I'm aware, no one has crossed the Sahara on a pogo stick. This could be a real opportunity. Anyone want to sponsor me?

A   The maestro of this new strategy is David Hempleman-Adams, who made a fortune from glue and then used his millions to stick together old challenges done years ago to make a new, big one – which he sold to national newspapers and a broadcasting company.

B   Somewhat at odds with this, they then go on to write the inevitable book based on the trip's hairier moments. There's quite a living to be made, I'm told, ghost writing for those amongst the intrepid who find their stamina flagging a little when faced with a blank page and a tight deadline.

C   In 1947, for example, Thor Heyerdahl sailed the Pacific Ocean in his balsawood boat, the Kon-Tiki, to repeat the voyage of South American Incas centuries before. Some fifty years later, the Spanish explorer Kitín Muñoz made a number of attempts to repeat that same crossing.

D   Their efforts are widely publicised by press releases and photo calls, but usually end up generating more stuff than they remove. Nevertheless, such an enterprise allows not only the participants, but also those back home to feel much better about themselves.

E   The Americans have a word for it – 'micro-distinction'. Everest may have been climbed a thousand times, but not by a pensioner without oxygen walking backwards and wearing a bobble hat. That challenge remains. The uncomfortable truth for latter-day explorers is that getting to the world's more remote corners is no longer that difficult.

F   No exploit is quite so outlandish, however, as that of the team from Idaho who were desperate to bring attention to the plight of the sockeye salmon, a fish whose numbers have fallen dramatically in recent years. They slithered 739 kms down the Snake River, imitating the journey of the juvenile salmon, which has become, according to their human champions, more hazardous than it used to be.

G   He gets my vote as, unlike most modern 'explorers', he understood the value of his achievement. 'It was ridiculous,' he later said. 'That's why I did it, and I wanted the publicity.'

Part 3

You are going to read a newspaper article. For questions **13–19**, choose the answer (**A, B, C** or **D**) which you think fits best according to the text. Mark your answers **on the separate answer sheet**.

BRIDGES

The Bosphorus Bridge in Istanbul links Europe to Asia. If you are standing in the middle of it, then what continent are you in? No, it's not a brainteaser with a quick answer; it's a question which hints at the fact that bridges are more complicated things than mere ways of getting from A to B. Dr Iain Borden researches psychological aspects of architecture at London University. 'Unlike going through a doorway, crossing a bridge takes time. While you are crossing the bridge, you are in neither one place nor the other but in a strange kind of limbo state,' he explains.

It may sound a little far-fetched, but Dr Borden's view is tapping into our fundamental responses to the physical world around us. The Ancient Britons attached great spiritual significance to rivers and certainly appreciated this concept of limbo. Recently a team from the Museum of London excavated the remains of the oldest bridge found so far in Britain (about 3,500 years old), in central London. In those days the River Thames was merely a collection of shallow channels and small islands. These islands had enormous spiritual resonance as places separated from the shores and connected to the river. But it is still true today that bridges are more than utilitarian structures and have a great symbolic impact.

'Bridges are associated with boundaries – social as well as physical,' says Dr Borden. 'When we cross a bridge we pass over some hazard or obstacle, but also over a threshold into a city, a different region or even a different country.' This is deliberately reflected in the way a bridge is designed to look open and welcoming, or forbidding and imposing; it can be celebrating the joining of two communities, or it can be holding them at arm's length. The bridge therefore exists on two levels: one physical, one political, and the two are linked. When a bridge is built where there was none before, it connects two places. Physically it makes trade and movement easier; psychologically the increased contact makes 'the other side' seem less distant. The bridge stands as a concrete representation of both the joining and the separation of two communities.

In a sense, the engineer designs the physical bridge and the architect designs the 'political' bridge. But, of course, it's not as simple as that. Sometimes, for example, the fact that a great engineering feat has been performed is itself an important statement. Furthermore, we have an innate aesthetic sense, which makes us like well-proportioned, stable structures. Engineers are not especially encouraged to consider visual impact, but good engineering can look quite attractive because it is balanced. Similarly, an architect with a good eye will often design a structure which is naturally stable. There is a great link between structure and form – overly whimsical or eccentric architecture is no longer beautiful or pleasing to the eye.

A bridge is peculiarly defined by its location – a power station will perform the same function wherever it is located, but a bridge joins two points – it cannot join them somewhere else. Various experts confirm the necessity of recognising this view. Lorenzo Apicella, a leading architect, says, 'You can't start to imagine what a bridge should look like until you know what it is joining together and what the surroundings are.' Neil Thomas, an engineer who has worked on many recent bridges, says, 'Each bridge presents a novel engineering problem. A bridge over a road or railway is very different from a bridge over a steep gorge where you can't build supports underneath.'

If a bridge is a product of its place, defined by what it is joining together or crossing over, it is also a product of its time. In the 19th century, the first European iron and steel bridges were built. Big, solid, metal structures marched across the landscape, metaphors for the triumph of human engineering in the Industrial Revolution over the agrarian past. The Romans, in a similar spirit, built aggressively solid roads and bridges wherever they went. They constructed an unprecedented communications and supply network, both physically and symbolically subduing the lands they marched across.

So what of today's bridges? Two of the longest suspension bridges in the world, both comparatively new, are the Great Belt Bridge in Denmark and the Akashi-Kaikyo bridge in Japan. Both link offshore islands (the latter to the mainland) and are part of larger road projects. Within Europe, the European Union is spending billions funding an integrated transport network. The dramatic increases in long-haul travel have fuelled an obsession with instant global accessibility. It seems as if we no longer want to savour the remoteness those Ancient Britons so treasured on their islands in the Thames.

13   What point is the writer making in the first paragraph?

    A   Bridges have a significance beyond their basic physical function.
    B   The impact of a bridge varies from country to country.
    C   The popular view of what bridges represent has changed.
    D   People have different reactions when crossing a bridge.

14   What does the writer say in the second paragraph about Dr Borden's interpretation of bridges?

    A   It is contradicted by basic physical laws.
    B   Our ancestors would have disagreed with it.
    C   Some people might think it is rather improbable.
    D   It does not really explain why the first bridges were built.

15   In the third paragraph the writer says that the design of a bridge

    A   can be a cause of conflict between the two communities it is connecting.
    B   must be clear in its delineation of the boundary between the two sides.
    C   should always have safety as its overriding concern.
    D   may be influenced by the need for a symbolic message.

16   What does the writer say in the fourth paragraph about the visual impact of a bridge?

    A   It is increasingly a matter which an engineer must consider.
    B   It is fundamentally unattractive if the design is unbalanced.
    C   It is affected by the bridges we are accustomed to.
    D   It is influenced surprisingly little by the shape of the bridge.

17   In the fifth paragraph, the writer says that people involved in bridge design need to

    A   examine reliable, standardised designs before they proceed.
    B   make an initial assessment of the site.
    C   consider whether a bridge is the best solution.
    D   be able to visualise the completed bridge's appearance from the outset.

18   The writer mentions the bridges of the Industrial Revolution and the Romans to show that

    A   bridges represent the spirit of the age in which they were built.
    B   bridges have been a mark of all sophisticated civilisations.
    C   bridges are not always beneficial in their effect on humanity.
    D   bridges that are technologically advanced are not confined to the modern era.

19   According to the writer, the Danish and Japanese bridges exemplify

    A   international co-ordination in bridge building.
    B   the current desire for easy worldwide travel.
    C   the modern preference for road transport over other forms of travel.
    D   the willingness of modern governments to invest heavily in profitable projects.

Part 4

You are going to read a magazine article about the rock band Franz Ferdinand and its website. For questions **20–34**, choose from the sections (**A–E**). The sections may be chosen more than once.

Mark your answers **on the separate answer sheet**.

Which section mentions the following?

the way the band divided up responsibility for aspects of the site content	20
positive reviews of the band's musical output	21
the shortcomings of some websites featuring other bands	22
the website giving users exclusive access to certain tracks	23
the band's level of satisfaction with the style of its website	24
website entries being both thoughtful and entertaining	25
the role of established business methods in the band's success	26
the technology behind the band's flexible use of its website	27
a band member seeing the potential in a professional relationship	28
the pioneers in a new approach to rock band websites	29
the role of the band's outward appearance in gaining them popularity	30
an acceptance that other websites were superior in certain respects	31
the website fitting in with the band's established image	32
a change in the general perception of acceptable website content	33
the difficulty a band member had in making regular contributions to the site	34

A Band and its Website

An innovative website helped transform Franz Ferdinand from a Glasgow club act into a national award-winning rock band.

A

In early 2004, the rock group Franz Ferdinand got their first big break when their second single 'Take Me Out' reached the British Top 10. A year later, they were collecting awards for the best rock act and the best British band, having gained both critical and popular acclaim for their debut album, and set up their own website. Indeed, Franz Ferdinand and their management attributed their success to more than sharp haircuts, natty outfits and the songs themselves. They believe that while their success was in part due to the tried-and-tested marketing techniques that make a new band – touring the music venues, relying on the build-up of business by word-of-mouth and convincing radio stations to play their stuff – it was also due in no small part to the internet.

B

Ever since the Web became a mass-market phenomenon in the late 1990s, record labels had largely been using it as just another marketing tool. For their biggest acts, they would build hugely expensive sites that acted as little more than moving billboards, leaving everything else to fan sites. Franz Ferdinand were different. They were amongst a new wave of popular bands who used the medium to bridge the gap between themselves and their fans. Groups like Radiohead started the trend, allowing internet users to watch them in the studio and share their innermost thoughts via online diaries. Franz Ferdinand took things a step further. They regularly appeared on their own message boards, chatting indiscriminately to fans and posting diary entries and photos from wherever they were in the world, using their own digital cameras, microphones and laptops. All four group members had access to the site's content-management system, making it easy for them to update it themselves.

C

The diary entries from lead singer Alex Kapranos, by turns amusing and insightful, were written on the road, giving them the quality of a freewheeling blog. Detailing a trip to France, for example: 'We played the amphitheatre in Lyon with PJ Harvey tonight. I split my trousers on stage, but it turned out not to be quite as tragic as it could have been,' he wrote, before going on to explain how a quick change and an extra long intro to the first song saved his blushes. This 'do-it-yourself' ethic is something that set the new breed of net-aware bands apart from their predecessors, according to Chris Hassell, new media director of DS Emotion, the company behind the site, who explains that what previously 'would have been seen as a bit geeky' was suddenly cool.

D

Hassell, who co-founded DS Emotion, the Leeds-based web design agency, says the band were heavily involved from the beginning. It was bass player Bob Hardy who noticed the work that the agency had done for another band and asked them to get involved. 'They had a very clear idea what the site should be like,' Hassell says, adding that they wanted the look that they had used on their sleeve designs and videos to be reflected in the site. As Alex Kapranos remembers: 'We were delighted with it. We gave them an aesthetic outline and they brought it to life. It was really easy to maintain. Bob was in charge of images and I wrote in the regular diary. I didn't always have access to a PC, but I tried to update it whenever I could.'

E

It wasn't long before the team behind the website was joined by a full-time news editor who regularly talked to all four members of the band, their management and their record label Domino to share ideas. 'We knew we couldn't compete with the fan sites in terms of the sheer amount of information on the band. They were doing that job very well. So we concentrated on things they couldn't do.' Hassell says that the online shop integrated into the site, for example, allowed the band to release material that would otherwise go unheard. By the time the band geared up to record its second album, DS Emotion was also working on a thorough overhaul of the website.

PAPER 2 WRITING (1 hour 30 minutes)

Part 1

You **must** answer this question. Write your answer in **180–220** words in an appropriate style.

1 You and your friend Alex are looking for a holiday job in the UK.

Read the note from Alex and the two adverts below. Then, **using the information appropriately**, write a letter to Alex, comparing the two jobs, saying which job you think is more suitable and giving reasons for your opinions.

> Hi,
> I've found these 2 job ads for holiday work. It'd be good to practise our English and do some sightseeing while we're in England. Both jobs look interesting – which do you think would be better for us?
>
> Alex

Joe's Italian Restaurant
Tel: 0207 876 2387
Staff needed for our restaurant
• Central London
• Friendly international staff
• Basic pay, plus tips
• Help finding accommodation

Tall Trees Campsite

014526 353545

Do you like meeting new people?
We need people to help organise the entertainment on our campsite.

- Popular British holiday resort
- Surrounded by beautiful countryside
- Good rates of pay
- Free accommodation

Write your **letter**. You should use your own words as far as possible. You do not need to include postal addresses.

Part 2

Write an answer to **one** of the questions **2–5** in this part. Write your answer in **220–260** words in an appropriate style.

---

2   You see the following notice in the local library.

> The *International Educational Development Agency* is collecting information about schools in different countries. The idea is to share this information to improve education in schools around the world.
> Please help us by writing a report on schools in your country. Your report should:
> • describe a typical school in your country
> • outline the strengths of typical schools in your country
> • suggest what could be done to improve schools in your country.

Write your **report**.

3   In class, you have been discussing family life. Your teacher has asked you to write an essay discussing the advantages and disadvantages of different generations of one family living together in the same house.

Write your **essay**.

4   You see this announcement in an international lifestyle magazine.

> People give each other presents for lots of different reasons. We'd like you, our readers, to give us your answers to these questions about present-giving:
>
> Why do we give presents – is it because we really want to or because of commercial or social pressures on us? What makes a good present?
>
> We'll publish the best articles in our next issue.

Write your **article**.

5   Answer **one** of the following two questions based on **one** of the titles below.

(a)   *The Pelican Brief* by John Grisham

You see this announcement on the internet and decide to write a review of *The Pelican Brief*.

> Many thrillers are pure fantasy and could never have happened in real life. We would like you, our readers, to send in a review of a thriller. Explain whether you think the plot is realistic, give reasons for your opinions and say if you would recommend this thriller to our readers.

Write your **review**.

(b)   *Lucky Jim* by Kingsley Amis

You have decided to write a review of *Lucky Jim* for your college magazine. In your review describe an event from *Lucky Jim* which you think is funny, and say how this event affects the rest of the story. Also say whether you think other people would enjoy *Lucky Jim*.

Write your **review**.

PAPER 3   USE OF ENGLISH (1 hour)

Part 1

For questions **1–12**, read the text below and decide which answer (**A, B, C** or **D**) best fits each gap. There is an example at the beginning (**0**).

Mark your answers **on the separate answer sheet**.

Example:

0 A demolition   **B** desolation   **C** destruction   **D** destitution

0	A	B	C	D
	⬜	⬜	⬛	⬜

Rowling's promise to save forests

The popular writer J K Rowling has agreed to end her part in the **(0)** .... of the world's forests by having her books printed on paper which is environmentally friendly. The multi-millionaire author, whose novels about a teenage wizard have **(1)** .... 6.5 million trees so far, is one of a number of high-profile authors who have **(2)** .... their support for the environment by stipulating that only recycled paper should be used for their books. Techniques **(3)** .... in Canada mean that, for the first time, paper made from such materials as office waste paper can be used to make books. The Canadian edition of Rowling's last book was printed without chopping down a single tree, saving an **(4)** .... 40,000 of them.

In the past, it was difficult to print books on recycled paper because the paper was not strong enough to **(5)** .... a lifetime's reading. Technological **(6)** .... mean that paper which is **(7)** .... from waste material is now just as **(8)** .... as paper made from virgin fibre in **(9)** .... of quality and strength.

Despite the high cost of developing recycled paper that has the required strength and whiteness needed for books, there will not **(10)** .... be a price rise for the reader. Instead, publishers are likely to **(11)** .... for the higher paper cost by using cheaper book covers, as **(12)** .... in Canada.

1   **A**   exhausted   **B**   erased   **C**   consumed   **D**   absorbed

2   **A**   contracted   **B**   pledged   **C**   secured   **D**   undertaken

3   **A**   founded   **B**   inaugurated   **C**   led   **D**   pioneered

4   **A**   estimated   **B**   assessed   **C**   established   **D**   evaluated

5   **A**   experience   **B**   withstand   **C**   confront   **D**   encounter

6   **A**   findings   **B**   gains   **C**   creations   **D**   advances

7   **A**   manufactured   **B**   constructed   **C**   devised   **D**   formed

8   **A**   firm   **B**   durable   **C**   persistent   **D**   substantial

9   **A**   provisions   **B**   concerns   **C**   terms   **D**   relations

10 **A**   certainly   **B**   naturally   **C**   absolutely   **D**   necessarily

11 **A**   balance   **B**   compensate   **C**   return   **D**   refund

12 **A**   developed   **B**   arose   **C**   happened   **D**   followed

Part 2

For questions **13–27**, read the text below and think of the word which best fits each gap. Use only **one** word in each gap. There is an example at the beginning (**0**).

Write your answers **IN CAPITAL LETTERS on the separate answer sheet.**

Example:

0	A																	

Truffles

The rarest and most expensive types of mushrooms in the world are called truffles and are considered **(0)** .... great delicacy. **(13)** .... the mushrooms we eat most of the time, **(14)** .... grow above the ground, truffles grow underground in natural woodland. They have a lumpy, irregular shape and vary **(15)** .... the size of a walnut to the size of a man's fist. **(16)** .... date, no one has been able to cultivate truffles. They grow wild and have to be hunted for. However, **(17)** .... to the commercial value of truffles, in most countries it is not possible to hunt for them **(18)** .... you have a licence to do so.

Ripe truffles produce a characteristic odour. If harvested before this odour develops, the truffle will not be mature **(19)** .... to eat. Only when it is fragrant is it truly flavourful. It is therefore **(20)** .... surprise that it is the smell of the truffle that leads the hunter to the right place. Dogs, with their keen noses, have been entrusted **(21)** .... the responsibility of truffle hunting. After **(22)** .... , a dog's sense of smell is up to 10,000 times better than **(23)** .... of a human. Almost **(24)** .... dog can be trained to seek out the valuable fungus by first learning to retrieve balls, then cheese, before **(25)** .... introduced to the truffle.

Pigs are also used to hunt truffles, but they are **(26)** .... from ideal. **(27)** .... they can successfully seek out and locate the truffle, they often eat it too.

Part 3

For questions **28–37**, read the text below. Use the word given in capitals at the end of some of the lines to form a word that fits in the gap **in the same line**. There is an example at the beginning (**0**).

Write your answers **IN CAPITAL LETTERS on the separate answer sheet**.

Example:

| 0 | A | B | I | L | I | T | Y | | | | | | | | |

Mahler's Fourth Symphony

The American conductor Michael Tilson Thomas has a rare (**0**) ....   **ABLE**

He can make all kinds of classical music (**28**) .... to a wide audience.   **ACCESS**

He (**29**) .... believes in bringing music to life in a way that can be enjoyed by   **PASSION**

everyone. Listeners will not be disappointed with his latest CD, which should

find a place among the truly great (**30**) .... of Mahler's Fourth Symphony. The   **RECORD**

opening theme is played at a pace which is (**31**) .... slow, but this proves to   **EXPECTED**

be (**32**) .... moving. Throughout the piece, there is an impression of perfect   **SURPRISE**

harmony and this makes listening extremely pleasurable.

The technical perfection of the performance demonstrates the (**33**) ....   **EXCEPTION**

high standard of musicianship reached by every member of the orchestra,

and the clarity of their playing (**34**) .... the listeners' musical experience.   **RICH**

The (**35**) .... of the soloists is especially impressive. The solo horn in   **EXPERT**

particular is truly (**36**) .... and manages to catch the conversational nature   **MEMORY**

of the music beautifully. Laura Claycomb sings the finale with exactly the

right tone of (**37**) .... and charm, and reminds us that this music is about   **SIMPLE**

dreams – of youthful innocence, of perfect happiness and peace.

Part 4

For questions **38–42**, think of **one** word only which can be used appropriately in all three sentences. Here is an example (**0**).

Example:

0 They say the new minister is a lovely person and very .... to talk to.

My neighbours have not had a very .... life, but they always seem cheerful.

It's .... enough to see why the town is popular with tourists.

Example: | 0 | E | A | S | Y | | | | | | | | | | | | | |

Write **only** the missing word **IN CAPITAL LETTERS on the separate answer sheet**.

---

38 TV and radio stations .... all the games in the tournament.

I thought the amount I paid .... postage as well as the cost of the books.

Chris .... his eyes with his hands when he realised the mistake he had made.

39 The article was criticised for giving a .... impression of life in the city.

The rumours about a tax increase were dismissed by the government as being totally ....

The police soon discovered that the man they had arrested was using a .... ID.

40 My brother was pleased when his company transferred him to the overseas ....

One .... of Patrick's family was descended from the kings and queens of Ireland.

The traffic had to be diverted when a huge .... fell and blocked the road.

41 I wouldn't describe myself as a sentimental person but this film, which is based on a true story, ... me deeply.

It was a very short interview, so the politician only .... on a couple of points that I was interested in.

Exhibits in the museum which may be .... by visitors are clearly labelled.

42 Because of where she'd been standing, Magda was able to give the journalist a full .... of the accident.

I'd love to stay with you for the weekend, but please don't go to a lot of trouble on my ....

If you're thinking of buying a new car, you need to take a number of factors into ....

Part 5

For questions **43–50**, complete the second sentence so that it has a similar meaning to the first sentence, using the word given. **Do not change the word given.** You must use between **three** and **six** words, including the word given. Here is an example (**0**).

Example:

0 James would only speak to the head of department alone.

ON

James .... to the head of department alone.

The gap can be filled with the words 'insisted on speaking', so you write:

Example: | **0** | INSISTED ON SPEAKING

Write **only** the missing words **IN CAPITAL LETTERS on the separate answer sheet**.

---

43 At the time, scientists did not realise how important their findings were.

FAILED

At the time, scientists .... of their findings.

44 People believe that Leonardo da Vinci foresaw the invention of aircraft.

BELIEVED

The invention of aircraft .... foreseen by Leonardo da Vinci.

45 Mr Porter has to lock all the doors at night after everyone has left.

RESPONSIBLE

The person who .... all the doors at night after everyone has left is Mr Porter.

46 Jack was worried that he couldn't think of any new ideas for the advertising campaign.

INABILITY

What worried Jack .... up with any new ideas for the advertising campaign.

47 The pool closes in ten minutes, so there isn't enough time to go swimming now.

WORTH

It .... now as the pool closes in ten minutes.

48 Pavel's advice helped me so much that I was able to solve the problem immediately.

SUCH

Pavel .... that I was able to solve the problem immediately.

49 Because she postponed buying the plane ticket, Vanessa lost the opportunity to go to China.

PUT

If Vanessa .... the plane ticket, she wouldn't have lost the opportunity to go to China.

50 Now the tourists have seen how beautiful it is here, there's a very good chance they'll return.

HAVING

The tourists are highly .... how beautiful it is here.

PAPER 4   LISTENING (approximately 40 minutes)

Part 1

You will hear three different extracts. For questions **1–6**, choose the answer (**A, B** or **C**) which fits best according to what you hear. There are two questions for each extract.

Extract One

You hear a reporter talking to a scientific illustrator at an exhibition of his work.

1 How did the illustrator feel when he began his work?

   A motivated to learn new computer techniques

   B confident he would attract commissions

   C keen to promote less popular species

2 What is the reporter's impression of the exhibition?

   A It is thoughtfully displayed.

   B It is comprehensive.

   C It is easy to locate.

Extract Two

You hear two journalists, Catherine and Tomas, talking about their work.

3 They agree that their new editor recognises their need

   A to have fewer meetings.

   B to balance work and family life.

   C to write about what interests them.

4 According to Tomas, how has the work of journalists changed over the last 20 years?

   A They find it easier to check their facts.

   B They are more likely to express their own views.

   C They treat the reporting of news stories more seriously.

Extract Three

You hear part of an interview with a zoologist called Roger Bonham.

5   What has Roger been working on recently at a zoo?

   A a breeding programme

   B a survey of native species

   C a fund-raising campaign

6   To secure the future of wildlife in Britain, he believes it is important to

   A monitor the area of land available for wildlife.

   B run educational programmes for city children.

   C raise awareness of the effects of pollution.

Part 2

You will hear a woman called Jill Arthur giving a talk about walking across the Gobi Desert in Asia. For questions **7–14**, complete the sentences.

CROSSING THE GOBI DESERT

To get fit, Jill went speed-walking in London with a

| | **7** |

which measured her weekly improvement.

An impractical item Jill bought for the trip was a large

| | **8** |

which she didn't keep long.

In the desert, a | | **9** | kept Jill awake on the first night.

The food provided at the end of a day's walk included

| | **10** | and fruit.

The group found that they couldn't always use a

| | **11** | for communication.

Jill said that some sand shapes made by the wind looked like

| | **12** | to her.

Jill took some | | **13** | to give to local villagers as presents.

On her return, Jill was delighted that her | | **14** | won a prize.

Part 3

You will hear part of an interview with a singer-songwriter called Nick Chalke, who is talking about his career. For questions **15–20**, choose the answer (**A, B, C** or **D**) which fits best according to what you hear.

15   What has recently helped Nick to produce so much work in a short space of time?

    A   the thought of the potential income
    B   the opportunity to alter his image
    C   a sense of artistic freedom
    D   a change of instrument

16   Musicians who participated in the recording of Nick's work were unhappy about

    A   the delay in receiving their fee.
    B   faults in the computer equipment.
    C   the lack of time allocated by the studio.
    D   restrictions on the type of instrument allowed.

17   When he was offered a contract to work with younger pop singers, Nick felt

    A   dissatisfied with the terms of the agreement.
    B   unwilling to take his wife's advice about it.
    C   sure that it wouldn't be good for his career.
    D   worried about his ability to get the best deal.

18   What does Nick say about the concept of 'the blues'?

    A   It can exist outside music.
    B   It is easy to write songs about.
    C   It is a popular genre for performers.
    D   It provides a lucrative topic for music journalists.

19   When asked about writing songs, Nick says that he

    A   completes a song every morning.
    B   needs peace in order to compose.
    C   sometimes uses his children's ideas.
    D   is often inspired by his local scenery.

20   In Nick's view, what makes a good song?

    A   The audience can identify with it easily.
    B   The words and music are completely original.
    C   The melody is one that people will remember easily.
    D   The words and music come to the songwriter at the same time.

Part 4

You will hear five short extracts in which people are talking about their jobs.

TASK ONE

For questions **21–25**, choose from the list (**A–H**) the reason each speaker gives for choosing their current job.

TASK TWO

For questions **26–30**, choose from the list (**A–H**) the problem each speaker encounters in their current job.

While you listen you must complete both tasks.

TASK ONE		TASK TWO	
A lack of prospects in a previous job		**A** co-operating with other employees	
B the fulfilment of a childhood dream	Speaker 1 **21**	**B** predicting suitable working conditions	Speaker 1 **26**
C interest in a particular hobby	Speaker 2 **22**	**C** time wasted filling in forms	Speaker 2 **27**
D the desire to gain a qualification	Speaker 3 **23**	**D** managing on a reduced income	Speaker 3 **28**
E the excitement of running risks	Speaker 4 **24**	**E** fitting work in with other commitments	Speaker 4 **29**
F strong family expectations	Speaker 5 **25**	**F** being short of living space	Speaker 5 **30**
G the opportunity to travel more widely		**G** working outside in bad weather	
H the chance to meet interesting people		**H** having to cope with long delays	

PAPER 5   SPEAKING (15 minutes)

There are two examiners. One (the interlocutor) conducts the test, providing you with the necessary materials and explaining what you have to do. The other examiner (the assessor) is introduced to you, but then takes no further part in the interaction.

Part 1 (3 minutes)

The interlocutor first asks you and your partner a few questions. The interlocutor asks candidates for some information about themselves, then widens the scope of the questions by asking about e.g. candidates' leisure activities, studies, travel and daily life. Candidates are expected to respond to the interlocutor's questions and listen to what their partner has to say.

Part 2 (a one-minute 'long turn' for each candidate, plus a 30-second response from the second candidate)

You are each given the opportunity to talk for about a minute, and to comment briefly after your partner has spoken.

The interlocutor gives you a set of pictures and asks you to talk about them for about one minute. It is important to listen carefully to the interlocutor's instructions. The interlocutor then asks your partner a question about your pictures and your partner responds briefly.

You are then given another set of pictures to look at. Your partner talks about these pictures for about one minute. This time the interlocutor asks you a question about your partner's pictures and you respond briefly.

Part 3 (approximately 4 minutes)

In this part of the test you and your partner are asked to talk together. The interlocutor places a new set of pictures on the table between you. This stimulus provides the basis for a discussion. The interlocutor explains what you have to do.

Part 4 (approximately 4 minutes)

The interlocutor asks some further questions, which leads to a more general discussion of what you have talked about in Part 3. You may comment on your partner's answers if you wish.

Test 2

PAPER 1   READING (1 hour 15 minutes)

Part 1

You are going to read three extracts which are all concerned in some way with television. For questions **1–6**, choose the answer (**A**, **B**, **C** or **D**) which you think fits best according to the text. Mark your answers **on the separate answer sheet**.

Extract from a novel

The interview

The world headquarters of 'FeetUpTV!' is a sort of shed in the suburbs. The guests on the programme I host, *Sharp Words*, tend to be old friends who want to do something to help me out, or former celebrities in a position not dissimilar to my own – hanging on but sinking fast. *Sharp Words* is two hours long, and though the advertising department, namely Karen on Reception, does its best, we are rarely interrupted by messages from our sponsors. The theoretical viewer (we keep up the pretence that someone is watching) is highly unlikely to feel that we have barely scratched the conversational surface.

I take pride in my interviewing. At a time when I seemed to be able to do nothing else properly, I hung on to my competence in a studio as I would to a tree root on the side of a cliff. I have conducted interviews with aggressive footballers and exaggerated actors. My studio sofa was my classroom, and I didn't tolerate any waywardness. I don't wish to overstate my case; it's not rocket science doing a TV interview. You chat to your guests beforehand, agree on a rough conversational course and remind them of their hilarious anecdotes. So when JJ and Jess came on as guests and decided that my programme was a joke and acted accordingly, I suffered something of a sense of humour failure. I wish, of course, that I could have found it in me to be a little less pompous, a little more relaxed.

1   What do we find out about the show *Sharp Words*?

   A   The company pays for celebrity guests from advertising revenue.
   B   The viewing figures tend to fluctuate depending on who the guests are.
   C   There isn't time for some guests to say everything they want to.
   D   Some guests come on the show out of sympathy for the presenter.

2   What does the writer imply about the interview with JJ and Jess?

   A   They did not treat the programme with the respect it deserved.
   B   He had not prepared them for the programme.
   C   They did not understand how difficult his job as an interviewer was.
   D   He no longer had the capacity to make people laugh.

TV criticism

A TV drama critic writes, 'It just wasn't really my thing.' It is impossible to imagine a respected literary, film or theatre critic writing like this. Television critics have no distinctive critical language, either borrowed or created. No television critic makes connections between television and larger culture in the way literary critics do. Programmes are reviewed as if they have no context, either in television or society at large. Of course, whereas some literary critics are writing about high literature for an educated audience, television critics can't assume the same kind of specialist knowledge. But then look at the references in rock music or film reviews. These critics are not unintelligent and they don't assume their readers are.

For years, television was disregarded by serious newspapers and academics. It was too ephemeral, too trivial. That debate is over. Half a century of great programmes has killed the condescension. Television has been central to the lives of two generations, and yet the gap between the importance – at times the greatness – of the medium, and the banality of the newspaper reporting is still staggering.

3 The writer mentions rock music and films because their critics

    A are looked down on in the same way that TV critics are.

    B show more respect for their audiences than TV critics do.

    C have borrowed techniques from literary criticism.

    D take into consideration the fact that they are writing for a wide audience.

4 What point is the writer making in the second paragraph about the situation today?

    A TV plays too great a part in most people's lives.

    B Newspaper critics feel some TV programmes are not worth commenting on.

    C The popularity of TV means programmes can never be treated seriously.

    D TV does not get the right type of coverage in newspapers.

Review of the book *Teen TV* (a collection of essays)

One of the biggest problems in writing about television, within a scholarly framework, is the rapid obsolescence of most programmes. The object of study keeps sliding away in television's relentless search for new formats. However, television does have a rich history, and we should not presume that only current programming is worthy of our attention.

Caution is advised, however, when writing about teen culture. Why is the emphasis in this collection of essays not on the popular reality-television formats? What is a 'teen' these days? A great deal more is needed on how the 'teen phenomenon' is exploited and what appeals to this demographic group. The nature of academic media enquiry means that researchers are usually investigating audience demographics and taste formations which rarely match their own. This is inevitable, and one should not adjudicate on whether the writers of this collection have got teenagers right or wrong. Their aim was to avoid the mistakes of earlier academic work on teen television, which, they argue, 'either praised and championed the chosen objects of study, or condemned their ideological dangers'. This collection largely avoids this, even though there is a strong tendency towards praise rather than condemnation. The strongest articles pay less attention to what a TV sitcom character said or did, and more to how such dramas draw on changing notions of teen identity.

5   What point is made about TV programmes in the first paragraph?

   A   It is impossible to compare past programmes with those of today.
   B   The lifespan of programmes tends to be brief.
   C   There are few programmes worthy of scholarly study.
   D   It is difficult to get viewers interested in new approaches.

6   In the second paragraph, the reviewer suggests that the writers who contributed to the book

   A   are more positive than negative about programmes aimed at teenagers.
   B   concentrate on analysis of TV characters when investigating the interests of teenagers.
   C   have close parallels in their own lives with those of the teenagers they write about.
   D   make the same errors as previous writers who have produced similar studies.

Part 2

You are going to read an extract from a newspaper article about ocean noise. Six paragraphs have been removed from the extract. Choose from the paragraphs **A–G** the one which fits each gap (**7–12**). There is one extra paragraph which you do not need to use. Mark your answers **on the separate answer sheet**.

CALLS FROM THE DEEP

Far beneath the waves, mysterious sounds and eerie echoes reverberate around the globe. David Wolman asks what is going on down there.

The Earth's oceans are full of noise: boats, whales, submarines and earth tremors all add to the aquatic cacophony. The study of ocean acoustics has helped scientists to monitor whale communication and migration, pinpoint the locations of undersea volcanoes, and measure ocean temperature. Yet there's still a handful of noises that continue to baffle researchers. Some last just a few minutes, while others go on continuously for years at a time, and nobody knows for sure what causes them.

7

The data is then analysed by examining its characteristics as it arrives at different hydrophones. Christopher Fox, the director of the Acoustic Monitoring Project in Newport, Oregon, says most recordings from the deep are easily identified, because the resulting soundwave patterns are as individual as voice prints. It is possible to look at the characteristics of a soundwave and identify a blue whale, a boat, or even an earthquake. But other noises remain unidentified. Most of these have names that Fox came up with on a whim, such as Upsweep, Train and Bloop.

8

Take the strange noise called Upsweep, for example, a flat tone accompanied by rising tones. It was heard continually between 1991 and 1994, and was at its loudest during the last 15 months of this period. During decades of tuning in to the oceans, the US Navy had never heard this signal before.

9

Then, in 1996, geologists working on the island of Tahiti came up with the most plausible explanation so far. Emile Okal and Jacques Talandier used seismometers, normally used to measure earthquakes, to analyse Upsweep. They suspected the phenomenon was instead caused by a volcanic process. Although Upsweep's relatively pure tone didn't fit with the more varied sounds usually typical of such activity, they speculated that it came from the oscillation of some kind of bubbly liquid, perhaps sea water coming into contact with a large pool of lava. Okal and Talandier homed in on the source using readings from eight different directions, including SOSUS data provided by Fox.

10

Other puzzling sounds may have more straightforward origins. Many noises can be traced to weather and ocean currents, and Fox suspects these are also responsible for the sound known as Train, which resembles the rushing sound of a distant train.

11

And even those species which have been well monitored could still be responsible for a curious sound or two, because most research focuses on audible frequencies rather than on the lower frequencies that ocean hydrophones pick up.

12

There's one crucial difference, however: in 1997 this sound was detected by sensors 4,800 kilometres apart. That means it must be far louder than any whale noise. Is it possible that some creature bigger than any whale is lurking in the ocean depths? Or, perhaps more likely, there is something that is much more efficient at making sound.

A A far more romantic possibility for the source of mystery noises is marine life. The sounds produced by many creatures haven't yet been catalogued, so little is known about their calls.

B The system that picks up all these sounds was established in the 1960s when the US Navy set up an array of underwater microphones, scattered around the globe. Known as SOSUS, short for Sound Surveillance System, these listening stations sit on the seabed at a depth where sounds can travel for thousands of kilometres, recording information.

C Fox also believes this. His hunch is that the sound nicknamed Bloop is most likely to come from some sort of animal, because its 'signature' is a rapid variation in frequency similar to that of sounds known to be made by marine animals.

D It was at first believed to be biological, possibly produced by fin whales. But when it was picked up by receivers on opposite sides of the Pacific, researchers concluded that it was too loud to have been produced by a whale. It also stayed the same over the course of many seasons, whereas whale song should have varied as the whales migrated.

E All this information pointed to a spot in the remote southern Pacific, roughly halfway between New Zealand and Chile. They radioed a French research ship in the region, which headed to the place and found that a previously identified chain of undersea mountains was in fact volcanic.

F The suggestion of a huge ocean creature raises a vision of a giant squid. There are no confirmed sightings of giant squid in the wild, although their bodies have been found on beaches. 'We don't have a clue whether they make any noise or not,' says Fox.

G These aren't meant to indicate the likely origins of the sounds, as no one knows what or who is responsible for them. But in a few cases the real cause may soon be identified.

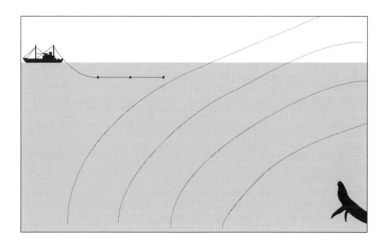

Part 3

You are going to read a newspaper article about an explorer. For questions **13–19**, choose the answer (**A, B, C** or **D**) which you think fits best according to the text. Mark your answers **on the separate answer sheet**.

THOR HEYERDAHL

It's more than 60 years since Thor Heyerdahl crossed the Pacific Ocean by raft. Shortly before Heyerdahl's death, Martin Buckley went to visit the legendary traveller, maverick scientist and reluctant hero.

Heyerdahl's home was a sprawling old villa in the remnants of an avocado plantation, saved from development by a local poet who once lived there, his privacy protected by tall trees and walls. The love of privacy was shared by Heyerdahl. With only the hastily hand-drawn map he had sent to me, I wandered the town for 45 minutes until the Heyerdahls' maid rescued me. At last, as I peered through a fence of barbed wire and cacti, I caught sight of the 84-year-old Heyerdahl coming to meet me. He stepped out of the shadows, slim, upright. It was a firm handshake.

'I'm sorry I'm so late,' I apologised, 'but this map is . . .'

'Oh, it's deliberate,' he said. 'Everyone is under orders to deny all knowledge of us – the police, shopkeepers. Even many of our own neighbours don't know we are here. I like to keep it that way.' He may have devoted his life to the solving of puzzles of place, but he delights in keeping his own location an enigma.

In 1947 Heyerdahl made the legendary Kon-Tiki expedition, in which he crossed the Pacific Ocean on a reconstructed prehistoric balsa-wood raft to prove that it was possible that the first Polynesians were immigrants from South America. 'After we made the Kon-Tiki expedition,' he told me, 'suddenly, all around the world, there were Kon-Tiki bars, Kon-Tiki restaurants – even Kon-Tiki matchbooks. It was difficult to know how to react.' But how did it feel to be the enduring object of so many projected dreams? 'It doesn't feel like that. I am amazed when people are excited to meet me. If you sit on a tiny raft at close quarters with people of all kinds for months on end, you learn that we are all fundamentally the same. What's more, I've never had the feeling that there's any positive consensus of opinion about me – I've been represented as a sort of tough sailor who's basically an ignorant madman. Some people may hero-worship me for Kon-Tiki, but I was pilloried for trying to put that theory forward. People said it should be silenced to death.'

The theory they tried to kill had started as the youthful Heyerdahl's notion that the inhabitants of certain Pacific Ocean islands had not – as academic orthodoxy held – migrated eastward from Asia. Such a voyage, Heyerdahl had noticed when investigating the region's oceanography, would be against the prevailing currents. Heyerdahl gradually became convinced that Polynesia's oldest inhabitants had travelled with the currents from – or via – South America on balsa-wood rafts. The American archaeologist Herbert Spinden had smiled patronisingly. 'Really – would *you* want to sail a balsa craft from Peru to Polynesia?'

'Well, maybe I will,' retorted Heyerdahl.

Half a hemisphere of water had to be negotiated, on an 11-metre craft made from nine balsa logs lashed together, with a grass-roofed hut on top. Six men and a parrot were crammed together on the small craft. They would cross the Pacific, they said, and they did; on 7 August 1947, 101 days after setting out, they made landfall. For months the world was agog at this tale of heroism on turquoise waters. Heyerdahl's book sold 20 million copies, and his documentary film won an Academy Award. The fates were smiling on him, it seemed. Then came the academic backlash. The crimes Heyerdahl stood accused of were twofold: first, poking his nose into another discipline (trained as a zoologist, how dare he dabble in archaeology?); second – and most outrageous – presenting an audacious theory to the public without submitting it to the academic hierarchy. Conferences were even convened to demolish his ideas.

'Do you feel bitter about it now?' I asked him. 'Perhaps if things had not gone the way they did, if I had not been able to prove my hypothesis, I would be bitter. But it left me with the conviction that there's something wrong with science. So much information is available nowadays that to make any forward progress you are forced to specialise, and any attempt at an overview is deemed impossible, and scorned, whereas I've always searched for the way things relate to each other. My real sadness is for the thousands of young people who are crushed by scientific orthodoxies before they even get a chance to advance their own ideas.'

For Heyerdahl, the wait for academic respectability was a long one. In his later years, though, acceptance began to come – albeit grudgingly. Authenticated finds of Greek and Roman artefacts in South America suggest that maritime connections across the oceans existed long before scientists had hitherto believed.

13 Why did the writer have such difficulty finding the Heyerdahls' home?

    A   He had purchased an inaccurate map.

    B   The entrance to the villa had been moved.

    C   Heyerdahl was keen to discourage visitors.

    D   Heyerdahl had been advised to conceal his whereabouts.

14 What did Heyerdahl realise in the course of his expedition?

    A   A common goal has a strong unifying effect.

    B   It is not easy to change people's long-held beliefs.

    C   One person is no more worthy of admiration than any other.

    D   You should follow your plans through, regardless of opposition.

15 What does Heyerdahl say about his fame?

    A   He feels uncomfortable with his reputation as a hero.

    B   There have always been conflicting views about him.

    C   He has never cared about negative opinions directed towards him.

    D   Most people have exaggerated the significance of his personal achievements.

16 What first led Heyerdahl to formulate his theory about the origins of the Polynesians?

    A   a desire to prove established scientists wrong

    B   his research into the practicalities of craft construction

    C   an investigation into early Asian influences on South America

    D   insights he gained from the study of non-archaeological evidence

17 Heyerdahl's greatest offence in the eyes of the established academics of the time was that he had

    A   shown disrespect towards an eminent archaeologist.

    B   failed to present his hypothesis to them.

    C   brought their discipline into disrepute.

    D   ridiculed their long-held beliefs.

18 Throughout his career, Heyerdahl tried to

    A   examine links between traditionally separate scientific fields.

    B   convince fellow scientists that his theory was the correct one.

    C   change the way that scientific discoveries are viewed by the public.

    D   persuade established academics to consider young scientists' ideas.

19 It took Heyerdahl many years to

    A   come to terms with his disappointments.

    B   achieve the scientific recognition he deserved.

    C   be offered an academic appointment.

    D   overcome feelings of resentment towards his critics.

Part 4

You are going to read a magazine article about the *Friends Reunited* website. For questions **20–34**, choose from the people (**A–D**). The people may be chosen more than once.

Mark your answers **on the separate answer sheet**.

Which person says this about their friend?

'I have a similarly demanding professional role to hers.'	20
'I accept that our personalities were never very compatible.'	21
'I am confident that our current friendship will be a lasting one.'	22
'I correctly predicted how successful she would become.'	23
'I am attracted by the idea that our earlier friendship might have endured.'	24
'I particularly appreciate a certain personality trait which we share.'	25
'I realise that our reunion has already been mutually beneficial.'	26
'I wouldn't have been able to predict her choice of career back then.'	27
'I remember the intensity of our short-lived original friendship.'	28
'I think that we'd have met again even without the help of the website.'	29
'I was rather taken aback by one decision that she'd made since we last met.'	30
'I regret having gradually lost contact with her before.'	31
'I had my doubts about the wisdom of meeting up.'	32
'Her choice of occupation confirms my earlier expectations.'	33
'It came as no surprise to me that she'd made a particular change.'	34

Old Friends Reunited

Friends Reunited is a website that helps old school and college friends find each other again after years apart. It has over eight million members and 15,000 new ones log on each day. Nigel Grey spoke to four people who have used the website.

A   Glenda Bisso, fashion writer, met her childhood friend Jane, now a costume designer.

'There's one significant difference since we last met; she's now called Cristiana professionally – I might've guessed she'd do something like that because she always longed to be rid of the name, but to me she looks exactly the same as she did then, and will always be Jane! I'd have recognised her anywhere. We were firm friends in those days despite the fact that she was an avid horse rider and I was somewhat wary of them. It's funny how we've ended up in remarkably similar careers, given that she was such a hearty outdoor child, but I suppose we had other things in common. Even so, I would never have imagined my world appealing to her – just shows that you should never pre-judge. I'd like to think we would've remained friends if my family hadn't moved away. Meeting up again held few fears for me as I'm quite a huggy, tactile person, and I'm sure our friendship can easily be permanently re-ignited.'

B   Verna Shingler, public relations advisor, met her teenage friend Ilona, now a nutritionist.

'Ilona and I belonged to a riotous youth club set: it was all practical jokes and her encouraging me to do things my parents would hardly have approved of. Then, when she was 18, she went to study in Italy and from then on was abroad most of the time. Sadly, we just drifted apart. We found each other on *Friends Reunited* and then, amazingly, before we'd even thought of a reunion, bumped into each other in a health food shop. I guess it was bound to happen sooner or later, as I'm always looking for supplements and Ilona is into natural healthcare professionally. At school she was always very focused and it's no great shock to me what she does for a living – the clues were all there at sixteen. I really hope she does well within the natural healthcare field – and that we become good friends again.'

C   Veronica Pringle, who works for a TV production company, met her old university friend Ella, now an assistant editor on a music magazine.

'We met in France, when working as language assistants. It was a remarkably close friendship that lasted the year we spent teaching. We holidayed together, met each other's families, but then our careers took us in different directions and I soon lost track of her – but I always felt close to her and wondered how she was. Ella was always very down-to-earth which I'm certainly not. I think I would have got on her nerves eventually and we'd have had a bust-up. It's better to have met again now, as adults. When we saw one another again for the first time, she seemed much more low-key. She was going through a rough patch and she's said that talking with me has been a catalyst for getting back on track. Working in TV makes you friendly with lots of people, and thanks to her I've become more discerning about choosing friends.'

D   Tamara Perry, a senior brand manager, met her childhood friend Katie, who now works as a technician at a catering equipment company.

'In twenty years, Katie doesn't appear to have aged at all! I was a bit disconcerted though to find she'd renounced her provincial accent in favour of a metropolitan one. We were friends from six until Katie moved from the area aged eleven. I went on the website as I was curious to know what had become of her. It had been such a long time that the reunion was daunting; how would we get on, if at all? I remember Katie having a strong personality and I spotted early on that she had the intellect and attitude to make a go of whatever she went in for. Although we each hold down challenging responsible posts with all that entails, we both have a mischievous streak, which I think is a real plus in life. I was pleasantly surprised that we still made each other laugh, although initially it was all about remembering old times and things we used to get up to. I can imagine that had we stayed in the same school, there might have been a time when we weren't as friendly as we were at eleven, but as adults we might've ended up as friends again. I'll definitely make the effort to keep in touch. I hope that she will too.'

PAPER 2   WRITING (1 hour 30 minutes)

Part 1

You **must** answer this question. Write your answer in **180–220** words in an appropriate style.

1   You are studying in the UK. A group of students from your college recently visited a studio where films are made. The film studio manager, Alison Riley, has written asking for your group's impressions of the day you spent there.

Read the extract from Alison Riley's letter below and the comments from students. Then, **using the information appropriately**, write a letter to Alison Riley explaining which aspects of the day you enjoyed and what you were disappointed by, and suggesting how future visits could be improved.

> It's the first time we've organised a visit to the studio and I'd be interested in what your group thought. Was there anything you didn't do or see that you'd like to have done or seen? Sorry we couldn't provide any lunch

Talk on studio history – boring

Not enough time to learn about lighting and sound

Best bit – meeting actors

Special effects – my favourite

Write your **letter**. You should use your own words as far as possible. You do not need to include postal addresses.

Part 2

Write an answer to **one** of the questions **2–5** in this part. Write your answer in **220–260** words in an appropriate style.

---

2   In class, you have been discussing the effects of mobile phones. Your teacher has asked you to write an essay on the following topic:

Young children should not be allowed to own mobile phones. To what extent do you agree?

Write your **essay**.

3   You recently saw the following announcement on the internet.

FREE LANGUAGE COURSE

The Worldwide Language Programme (WLP) is offering a prize of six months' free English language tuition in the country of your choice. Write to the institute and say which English-speaking country you would choose and why, how this experience could affect your future, and why you would be the most deserving winner. The most persuasive entry will receive the prize.

Write your **competition entry**.

4   You see the following in an international sports magazine.

Extreme Sports

We are looking for extreme sports fanatics to write an article for us. We'd like you to:
- tell us about one extreme sport that you would like to try, and explain why
- describe what type of person is attracted to extreme sports.

We will print the most interesting article.

Write your **article**.

5   Answer **one** of the following two questions based on **one** of the titles below.

(a)   *The Pelican Brief* by John Grisham

Your college library is planning to buy more thrillers and has asked you to write a report on *The Pelican Brief*. In your report describe what you think the ingredients of a good thriller are and say whether you think *The Pelican Brief* is a good thriller, giving your reasons.

Write your **report**.

(b)   *Lucky Jim* by Kingsley Amis

Your teacher has asked you to write an essay about relationships in *Lucky Jim*. In your essay, describe Jim's relationship with one of the other characters and explain why you think this relationship is interesting.

Write your **essay**.

PAPER 3   USE OF ENGLISH (1 hour)

Part 1

For questions **1–12**, read the text below and decide which answer (**A, B, C** or **D**) best fits each gap. There is an example at the beginning (**0**).

Mark your answers **on the separate answer sheet**.

Example:

0 A based   **B** centred   **C** built   **D** stationed

0	A	B	C	D
	▄▄	☐	☐	☐

A community choir

Open Voices is a community choir **(0)** .... in the town of Kingston, in Ontario, Canada. It was founded last year by a man called Andy Rush, an accomplished musician with a 16-year **(1)** .... record as a choir director.

Andy began by researching the way other community choirs were **(2)** .... , before deciding on the **(3)** .... he wished to use for his own choir. He then advertised for people to come and try out the choir. There were no auditions and a **(4)** .... in music was not necessary. The purpose of the trial session was simply to give people the opportunity to sing in a choir and get a **(5)** .... for the experience before making any **(6)** .... to it. In order to **(7)** .... the barriers that can prevent people from joining groups like this, he provided transportation, childcare, and subsidised membership fees for those who needed them. His goal was to make Open Voices inclusive and welcoming, and to **(8)** .... people from a variety of musical, cultural and social environments.

Andy expected 50 or 60 responses to his advertisement. In the event, 279 people **(9)** .... an interest in joining the choir. In order to **(10)** .... everyone, the choir had to be **(11)** .... into two groups, each one rehearsing on a different day. Open Voices has now held several **(12)** .... successful concerts and has many more planned for the future.

1	**A**	course	**B**	track	**C**	path	**D**	line
2	**A**	set down	**B**	set off	**C**	set up	**D**	set on
3	**A**	guide	**B**	model	**C**	sample	**D**	pattern
4	**A**	backup	**B**	backdrop	**C**	background	**D**	backlog
5	**A**	touch	**B**	mood	**C**	sense	**D**	feel
6	**A**	commitment	**B**	allegiance	**C**	dedication	**D**	assurance
7	**A**	overlook	**B**	overcome	**C**	overwhelm	**D**	overtake
8	**A**	catch on	**B**	pull up	**C**	take out	**D**	bring in
9	**A**	suggested	**B**	expressed	**C**	described	**D**	conveyed
10	**A**	accommodate	**B**	contain	**C**	arrange	**D**	maintain
11	**A**	torn	**B**	cut	**C**	sliced	**D**	split
12	**A**	fully	**B**	deeply	**C**	highly	**D**	greatly

Part 2

For questions **13–27**, read the text below and think of the word which best fits each gap. Use only **one** word in each gap. There is an example at the beginning (**0**).

Write your answers **IN CAPITAL LETTERS on the separate answer sheet.**

Example:

0	A	S																

An excellent writer

To the surprise of many people, Brutus is rapidly acquiring a reputation **(0)** .... an excellent writer of short stories. And why ever **(13)** .... ? He has shown he has the vocabulary, grammar and plot devices to write his most recent story, **(14)** .... which he has chosen the title *Betrayal*.

Amazingly, not **(15)** .... the best literary critics can easily tell the difference between Brutus's stories and those written by distinguished human authors, although Brutus, as you **(16)** .... surely have guessed by now, is a computer. Brutus produced his story for a competition in **(17)** .... human authors also participated – and he won! The four best stories were published on the internet, with readers being asked to identify the computer-written story. Only 25% of the people who took part got **(18)** .... right! This obviously means that Brutus **(19)** .... appear to satisfy the condition laid down by Alan Turing, the computer pioneer. Turing argued that once people could not tell **(20)** .... they were dealing with a computer or a human, then the computer must have achieved consciousness.

It has taken seven years to develop Brutus but **(21)** .... his achievements, he has a **(22)** .... limitations. Later versions of Brutus may do better but **(23)** .... far he cannot write anything longer than five hundred words. **(24)** .... is more, all his stories are written **(25)** .... a male point of view and all focus **(26)** .... people working at universities who are betrayed by colleagues. It **(27)** .... well be that this reflects the preoccupations of the scientists who programmed him.

Part 3

For questions **28–37**, read the text below. Use the word given in capitals at the end of some of the lines to form a word that fits in the gap **in the same line**. There is an example at the beginning (**0**).

Write your answers **IN CAPITAL LETTERS on the separate answer sheet**.

Example:

0	D	R	A	M	A	T	I	C									

The Indian monsoon

The Indian monsoon is a **(0)** .... weather phenomenon which begins in   **DRAMA**

June each year. After months of intense sunshine, the sky **(28)** .... as   **DARK**

the sun disappears beneath a blanket of cloud. Then, in an instant, sheets

of **(29)** .... rain pour onto the parched landscape. Over the next three   **TORRENT**

months, the monsoon will deliver as much as ninety per cent of the region's

yearly rainfall. It is a truly **(30)** .... phenomenon, but it is a mixed blessing   **SPECTACLE**

to the people of the region. **(31)** .... , many fear the inevitable floods, but   **DOUBT**

without the monsoon neither humans nor wildlife could survive.

David Stephenson and K Rupa Kumar are distinguished climatologists who

(32) .... in the study of the Indian monsoon. Together they maintain an   **SPECIAL**

(33) .... website on the subject. Dr Stephenson's aim is to predict with   **EXTEND**

greater **(34)** .... where and when the rain will fall. 'The importance of having   **ACCURATE**

reliable predictions cannot be overstated,' he explains. 'This is because

farmers need to know when to plant their crops to make the most **(35)** ....   **ADVANTAGE**

use of the rains.' Their forecasts are becoming **(36)** .... accurate, and the   **INCREASE**

climatologists are working **(37)** .... to improve them.   **CONTINUE**

Part 4

For questions **38–42**, think of **one** word only which can be used appropriately in all three sentences. Here is an example (**0**).

Example:

0 They say the new minister is a lovely person and very .... to talk to.

My neighbours have not had a very .... life, but they always seem cheerful.

It's .... enough to see why the town is popular with tourists.

Example:

0	E	A	S	Y														

Write **only** the missing word **IN CAPITAL LETTERS on the separate answer sheet**.

---

38 PD James's latest best-selling book is in the .... of being made into a film.

The .... of turning crude oil into plastic is very complex.

Ageing is a natural .... and we should not be afraid of it.

39 Tom .... a line under his work to show that it was completed.

The judge .... that the boy was too young to appear in court as a witness.

The king had .... his country for over fifty years and was much loved by his subjects.

40 They had to switch off the .... in the neighbourhood before they repaired the cables.

How long has this government been in .... ?

The chair of the committee has the .... to call an emergency meeting at short notice.

41 Ideally, newspapers should base their reports on .... facts, not rumours, but this doesn't always happen.

José had assumed that his agent would support him, so when she was critical, he found it .... to take.

People who live in Siberia are used to .... winters lasting several months.

42 I became suspicious when I .... the cleaner looking through the papers on my desk.

Sorry we're late but we got .... in a terrible traffic jam.

It took Milo a while but eventually he .... his teacher's attention.

Part 5

For questions **43–50**, complete the second sentence so that it has a similar meaning to the first sentence, using the word given. **Do not change the word given.** You must use between **three** and **six** words, including the word given. Here is an example (**0**).

Example:

0 James would only speak to the head of department alone.

ON

James ………………………………………………… to the head of department alone.

The gap can be filled with the words 'insisted on speaking', so you write:

Example:	**0**	INSISTED ON SPEAKING

Write **only** the missing words **IN CAPITAL LETTERS on the separate answer sheet**.

---

43 Dr Sharp wants you to look after his patients while he's away.

CARE

Dr Sharp would like you to …………………………………………………… his absence.

44 Yasmin's uncle said to her that she should stop her children eating junk food.

LET

Yasmin's uncle told her …………………………………………………… junk food any more.

45 I was surprised how hard I had to work when I became a teacher.

EXPECTED

I had to …………………………………………………… when I became a teacher.

46 We will send your new passport tomorrow, provided your paperwork is in order.

LONG

Your new passport will …………………………………………………… your paperwork is in order.

47 The weather was getting worse, so Joe was forced to give up his attempt to climb to the summit.

BUT

Due to the worsening weather, Joe had ……………………………………………………………… to give up his attempt to climb to the summit.

48 What are your plans for celebrating Nina's birthday?

MIND

What ……………………………………………………… for celebrating Nina's birthday?

49 Once the visitors had gone, Rachel started her homework immediately.

DOWN

Once the visitors had gone, Rachel immediately ………………………………………………………… her homework.

50 Pierre's presentation showed he was against the proposed takeover.

OBJECTED

In his presentation, Pierre made it …………………………………………………………… the proposed takeover.

PAPER 4   LISTENING (approximately 40 minutes)

Part 1

You will hear three different extracts. For questions **1–6**, choose the answer (**A**, **B** or **C**) which fits best according to what you hear. There are two questions for each extract.

Extract One

You overhear two friends, Bill and Maria, discussing a marathon race they are both going to run in.

1   They agree that the day before a race it's best to

   A   take some moderate exercise.

   B   have a rest.

   C   train in a gym.

2   What advice does Bill give Maria about the race itself?

   A   adapt her race plan according to how she feels

   B   avoid drinking too much water at the start

   C   run at a steady speed throughout

Extract Two

You hear part of a discussion in which two students are talking about their course in journalism.

3   What do they think makes the course particularly interesting?

   A   the mix of face-to-face and online sessions

   B   the enthusiasm of the lecturers

   C   the range of topics covered

4   What do they suggest is an increasing problem for journalists?

   A   the legal consequences of what they report

   B   the difficulty of finding stories to attract readers

   C   the decrease in sales of newspapers and magazines

Extract Three

You hear part of a radio programme about the types of books that people read.

5   How does the woman feel about her work-related reading?

    A frustrated by its level of difficulty

    B conscious of the demands it makes on her

    C concerned at the lack of satisfaction it gives her

6   The man likes reading books by authors who

    A are skilled at describing unusual characters.

    B put across ideas in a straightforward way.

    C concentrate on people's ordinary lives.

Part 2

You will hear a talk about the dogs that work in the Arctic. For questions **7–14**, complete the sentences.

ARCTIC DOGS

The dogs are famous for their qualities of [| **7**] and dependability.

Physically, the dogs have a deep [| **8**] and powerful shoulders.

The dogs' [| **9**] stay at a lower temperature than the rest of their body.

The dogs are attached to the line pulling the sled by [| **10**] and ropes.

The dogs that provide the power in the team are called [| **11**] dogs.

The older dogs usually go at the [| **12**] of the line.

The driver uses his [| **13**] to control the dogs.

To survive overnight in the huts, drivers need a [| **14**] as well as a fire.

Part 3

You will hear an interview with David McKinley, who recently opened 'The Adventure Centre', an adventure sports centre in Scotland. For questions **15–20**, choose the answer (**A**, **B**, **C** or **D**) which fits best according to what you hear.

15 David was first inspired to set up 'The Adventure Centre' when

    A he was working as a TV cameraman.
    B he was employed as a fitness instructor.
    C he was approached by an architect with the idea.
    D he analysed the potential profitability of the project.

16 David left the film industry because he found it too

    A insecure.
    B demanding.
    C competitive.
    D conventional.

17 When asked to sum himself up, David describes himself as

    A impulsive by nature.
    B over-critical of others.
    C prone to making mistakes.
    D lacking a natural business instinct.

18 David says that the most memorable period of his career involved

    A working on his own.
    B shooting a particular film.
    C watching something being built.
    D establishing his commercial reputation.

19 What does David think he will have difficulty with in the future?

    A retaining existing club members
    B educating people about their health
    C competing with other health and leisure clubs
    D encouraging more interest in adventure sports

20 What does David tell us about his customers?

    A They are becoming less physically active.
    B They are increasingly aware of their health needs.
    C They have grown bored with the range of sports traditionally offered.
    D They have unrealistic expectations about participation in adventure sports.

Part 4

You will hear five short extracts in which people are talking about taking a gap year – the time which some young people take off from their studies to gain other experience.

TASK ONE

For questions **21–25**, choose from the list (**A–H**) what each speaker did during their gap year.

TASK TWO

For questions **26–30**, choose from the list (**A–H**) the benefit of having a gap year which each speaker mentions.

While you listen you must complete both tasks.

A teaching a language	A making long-lasting friendships
B travelling widely	B generating essential income
C working in an office	C increased independence
D voluntary work	D improved linguistic skills
E teaching a sport	E learning to deal with disappointment
F working in a hotel	F a renewed sense of adventure
G working as a tour guide	G a more mature approach to studying
H going on an organised expedition	H a chance to consider future plans

Speaker 1	21		Speaker 1	26
Speaker 2	22		Speaker 2	27
Speaker 3	23		Speaker 3	28
Speaker 4	24		Speaker 4	29
Speaker 5	25		Speaker 5	30

PAPER 5   SPEAKING (15 minutes)

There are two examiners. One (the interlocutor) conducts the test, providing you with the necessary materials and explaining what you have to do. The other examiner (the assessor) is introduced to you, but then takes no further part in the interaction.

Part 1 (3 minutes)

The interlocutor first asks you and your partner a few questions. The interlocutor asks candidates for some information about themselves, then widens the scope of the questions by asking about e.g. candidates' leisure activities, studies, travel and daily life. Candidates are expected to respond to the interlocutor's questions and listen to what their partner has to say.

Part 2 (a one-minute 'long turn' for each candidate, plus a 30-second response from the second candidate)

You are each given the opportunity to talk for about a minute, and to comment briefly after your partner has spoken.

The interlocutor gives you a set of pictures and asks you to talk about them for about one minute. It is important to listen carefully to the interlocutor's instructions. The interlocutor then asks your partner a question about your pictures and your partner responds briefly.

You are then given another set of pictures to look at. Your partner talks about these pictures for about one minute. This time the interlocutor asks you a question about your partner's pictures and you respond briefly.

Part 3 (approximately 4 minutes)

In this part of the test you and your partner are asked to talk together. The interlocutor places a new set of pictures on the table between you. This stimulus provides the basis for a discussion. The interlocutor explains what you have to do.

Part 4 (approximately 4 minutes)

The interlocutor asks some further questions, which leads to a more general discussion of what you have talked about in Part 3. You may comment on your partner's answers if you wish.

Test 3

PAPER 1 READING (1 hour 15 minutes)

Part 1

You are going to read three extracts which are all concerned in some way with travel. For questions **1–6**, choose the answer (**A, B, C** or **D**) which you think fits best according to the text. Mark your answers **on the separate answer sheet**.

LIFE IN THE SLOW LANE

When I announced to my teenage children that I was taking off on a boat along Britain's canals for four months, they bought me a stripey jumper and an unfashionable waterproof jacket as brutal going-away presents. I withstood their arrows, and, within days of starting my 1,400-kilometre circumnavigation of the country, I was hooked. Eventually even my sceptical offspring got caught up in the spell as they joined up with me for different sections of the long trip.

Half the British population live within eight kilometres of an inland waterway, and yet many don't realise that if they hired a boat they'd slip through Britain's back door into a peaceful lost world. Water brings out the best in people. Someone who walks past you without a glance in a village will, 100 metres away, walking on the towpath alongside the canal, invariably smile, greet and maybe even offer to help you through the next lock gate. I returned home from my odyssey with a new faith in slow-time travel. And I actually rather like the jacket.

1   What do we learn about the writer and his children?

   A   His children did not believe that he would complete the journey.
   B   He tried hard to persuade his children to accompany him.
   C   His children changed their opinion of canal-boat travel.
   D   He did not understand his children's attitude towards his travel plans.

2   What does the writer say in the second paragraph about people and canals?

   A   People travelling by canal boat are reluctant to accept any help.
   B   People behave differently near canals to how they would behave elsewhere.
   C   The canal environment tends to attract a certain type of person.
   D   Canal-boat travellers usually act in a helpful way towards each other.

Website Review

mrparticular.com

Mr Particular (mrparticular.com) is an unnamed hotel reviewer who, in the best tradition of hotel reviewers, tours hotels in Britain while keeping his identity a closely guarded secret. His prose is sharp to the point of being barbed. Mr Particular is extremely particular. Indeed, he searches out faults and deficiencies with the appetite of a hungry wolf. But, he says, if you are paying close on a week's   *line 6*
wages to stay the night somewhere, then it jolly well ought to be up   *line 7*
to scratch.   *line 8*

Do we really need the likes of Mr Particular in an age when any hotel guest is capable of uploading their own reviews to the Internet? Well, yes, we probably do, because what Mr Particular brings to the table are three things you don't find on the usual post-your-own-opinions websites: obsessive detail, a lifetime of experience and an eloquent turn of phrase. However, there is a bug in the bed. The   *line 14*
thing about secret hotel reviews is that someone still has to foot   *line 15*
the bill. In this case, rather than a newspaper or the hotel itself, Mr   *line 16*
Particular is looking at you. For 52 reports a year he is asking for £104. On the one hand that's just £2 a week, but on the other, that's a night in a decent hotel.

3 Which phrase in the text suggests the writer's opinion about the service offered by the website?

  A a hungry wolf (line 6)
  B up to scratch (lines 7–8)
  C a bug in the bed (line 14)
  D foot the bill (line 15–16)

4 What does the writer of the text imply about the website?

  A It offers similar value for money to other sites.
  B Its reviews are no more informative than those on other sites.
  C Its reviews focus mainly on higher category hotels.
  D It may not be worth the fee charged to access it.

WALKING THE WORLD
Author's Introduction

Walking is a pace and movement suited to the human frame and temperament, giving one opportunity to think, while at the same time offering a type of physical exercise many of us seek but neglect. It has more benefits than aspirin and encourages the deepest and healthiest of sleep. Another advantage of putting one foot in front of the other is the financial one. Walking is an inexpensive method of moving around and, in our teeming cities, frequently the fastest. It can be a prelude to and reason for adventure, and I feel there is a sense of achievement that riding a mechanical vehicle will never offer when passing from A to B.

When I came to write this book I pondered long and seriously upon the desirability of a walking book pure and simple, or one covering progress maintained by other sets of legs – such as those belonging to the horse, camel, mule and elephant, plus, perhaps, the bicycle, on which one's own legs are used as a means of propulsion. I finally came down on the side of simple walking, since the scope of my foot-travels covers, if not a multitude of haunts for the walker, a wide enough one to awake the interest of readers. It is my hope that many of these may wish to follow my example and some, maybe, my footsteps.

5   What point does the author make about walking in the first paragraph?

   A   Many people do less walking than they would like to.
   B   Most people who walk in cities ignore the disadvantages.
   C   Many people believe walking is less healthy than other forms of exercise.
   D   Most people find walking more enjoyable than mechanised transport.

6   Why did the author decide against including other means of transport in his book?

   A   He believed he lacked first-hand knowledge of them.
   B   He doubted whether readers would be interested in them.
   C   He thought that it would be too broad a subject to deal with in one book.
   D   He felt that the extent of his walking experience was sufficiently inspiring.

Part 2

You are going to read an extract from a magazine article. Six paragraphs have been removed from the extract. Choose from the paragraphs **A–G** the one which fits each gap (**7–12**). There is one extra paragraph which you do not need to use. Mark your answers **on the separate answer sheet**.

The Birth of Spider-Man

Nick Drake reports on the origins of the comic-book superhero Spider-Man.

Spider-Man, the brainchild of writer Stan Lee, has been one of the world's most popular comic-book characters since he first climbed his way up a wall in 1962. Superman may be able to fly, and Batman may have neat gadgets, but Spider-Man has always been the superhero with style. Whether he's swinging from a high-rise office block or just trying to win his girl's heart, there's always been something irresistible about him, a quality which other comic-book strongmen have never matched.

7	

Indeed, it's a point made in a new book about the Marvel Comic Company and the characters it produced. He was neurotic, compulsive and profoundly sceptical about the idea of becoming a costumed saviour. His contemporaries, the Fantastic Four, argued with each other, and both The Hulk and Thor had problems with their alter egos, but Spider-Man alone struggled with himself.

8	

Born in New York in 1922, he joined the company when he was seventeen, working his way up through the firm until he was writing many of the titles. It wasn't until the early 1960s, however, that he gained the freedom to create many of the characters who would make his name. Stan recalls that a throwaway idea gave birth to one of the world's great superheroes.

9	

For months, Stan had been toying with the notion of a new superhero, one who would be more realistic than most, despite his colourful super-power. He has since confessed that he'd dreamt up the idea from watching a fly on the wall while he'd been typing.

He took the idea to his boss, the publisher Martin Goodman, telling him that he wanted to feature a hero whose main power was the fact that he could stick to walls and ceilings.

10	

Stan waited for the enthusiastic reaction, for a hearty pat on the back and a robust: 'Go for it!' But it didn't come. On the contrary, he was told that he was describing a comedy character, not a hero. Heroes are too busy fighting evil to slow down the stories with personal stuff.

11

So to get it out of his system, Stan gave famed Marvel artist Jack Kirby his Spider-Man plot and asked him to illustrate it. But when Stan saw that Jack was drawing the main character as a powerful-looking, handsome, self-confident hero, he took him off the project. Jack didn't mind – after all, Spider-Man wasn't exactly the company's top character.

12

Then they just forgot about it. But, some time later, when the sales figures came in, they showed that Spider-Man had been a smash success, perhaps the best seller of the decade! Stan laughs when he recalls Martin Goodman's priceless reaction: 'Stan, remember that Spider-Man idea that I liked so much? Why don't we turn it into a series?' Spider-Man went on to be one of the most successful characters in comic-book history.

A Stan then passed the assignment over to Steve Ditko, whose toned-down, highly-stylised way of drawing would, he thought, be perfect for Spider-Man. And he was right. Steve did a brilliant job in bringing the character to life. So they finished the comic strip and put it in that last edition, even featuring their new hero on the cover.

B Another innovation which this creative genius brought to comic books was one which enhanced the reader's grasp of the superhero's subjective viewpoint – the thought bubble.

C As the man responsible for creating not only this troubled character but also The Silver Surfer and many more, Stan Lee managed to transform the much maligned comic art form into a multi-million-dollar industry and turn Marvel Comics into a household name.

D The new hero would also be a teenager, with all the problems, hang-ups and angst that go with adolescence. He'd be a loser in the romance department. Except for his superpower he'd be the quintessential hard-luck kid.

E Marvel comics had just one comic-book title that didn't feature superheroes. Stan was producing the title, called *Amazing Fantasy*, which featured all sorts of brief, far-out comic strips. Stan loved it but sales were disappointing, so it was decided that he would do one last issue and then let it rest in peace.

F What's more, the name was a disaster. Didn't Stan realise that people hate spiders? But Stan couldn't get Spider-Man out of his head. That's when he remembered that final issue of *Amazing Fantasy* he was doing. He thought that no one would much care about what went into the last issue.

G The secret of Spider-Man's success was, in part, a depth of characterisation that readers had never before seen in such a protagonist. There isn't 'slam-bam-crash-boom' in every panel of a Spider-Man comic strip. Rather, the reader becomes privy to the hero's inner thoughts about his troubled life.

Part 3

You are going to read a magazine article. For questions **13–19**, choose the answer (**A**, **B**, **C** or **D**) which you think fits best according to the text. Mark your answers **on the separate answer sheet**.

Recreating sails used on Viking ships

The people known as the Vikings, from Norway, are famous for sailing round much of the world – but how did they do it? Nancy Bazilchuk investigates.

Since the middle of the 1800s, archaeologists have been studying a series of well-preserved Viking ships, excavated from grave mounds or raised from the bottom of narrow rivers leading to the sea. What they were missing were the ships' sails: such old cloth rarely survives in the environments that preserve wood. But after delving into old documents, Jon Godal and Eric Andersen from the Viking Ship Museum at Roskilde in Denmark decided old sails might be preserved elsewhere. They found a Viking law dating from about AD 1000 which stated: 'The man on whom responsibility falls shall store the sail in the church. If the church burns, this man is responsible for the sail …'. They struck it lucky in the church at Trondenes. Crammed between the walls and the roof was a fragment of woollen sail. It may once have been put in the church for safety.

Amy Lightfoot, head of the *Tommervik Textile Trust* in Hitra, Norway, had been studying coastal people's use of a tough, lanolin-rich wool to weave *vadmal*, a thick woollen cloth used to make durable clothing. When the Coastal Museum in Hitra decided in 1991 to build a replica of a boat used locally in the 1300s, it decided that it should have a woollen sail based on the fragment from Trondenes, and Lightfoot was chosen for the task. There was only one catch: the knowledge needed to produce such an object had perished with the sails themselves. 'But people still made *vadmal*, and we could talk to them about that,' says Lightfoot.

Even the simplest sail is a highly complex tensile structure. The fabric must be heavy enough to withstand strong winds, but not so heavy that it slows the ship. The trick to achieving this balance lies in the strength of the different threads, the tightness of their twist and their watertightness. The discovery of the Trondenes sail meant that these intricacies could be examined in Viking-age cloth. Analysis of the sail showed that its strength came from the long, coarse outer hairs of a primitive breed of northern European short-tailed sheep called *villsau*. These can still be found in Finland and Iceland. They do not need shelter in winter, as their wool is saturated with water-repellent lanolin. The quality of their wool owes much to their diet, which is new grass in summer and heather in winter. Historical and radiocarbon data from as early as 1400 BC show that Norwegian coastal farmers burnt the heather every year in spring. This kept down the heather and it also prevented the invasion of young pine trees that would eventually turn the farmers' grazing land to forest. The *villsau* thrived on the summer grass and in fact helped to encourage its growth. The flocks gained enough weight to survive on heather over the winter.

When it came to making a sail for the Coastal Museum's boat, the *Sara Kjerstine*, Lightfoot was able to provide a limited amount of *villsau* wool from a flock of 25 sheep she kept herself. The remainder came from a modern relative called the *spelsau.* Both types of wool had to be worked by hand to preserve the lanolin and to separate the long, strong outer hairs from the weaker, inner wool. This was not a trivial undertaking: the *Sara Kjerstine* required an 85-square-metre sail that consumed 2,000 kilograms of wool, a year's production from 2,000 sheep. It took Lightfoot and three helpers six months to pull the wool from the *villsau*. Spinning the wool into 165,000 metres of yarn and weaving the sail took another two years.

In 1997 Lightfoot joined forces with the Viking Ship Museum at Roskilde. They wanted a woollen sail for a replica they were building of a cargo ship. This time Lightfoot took a short cut: instead of pulling out the wool, it was sheared. Nevertheless, as Lightfoot spent endless hours working the wool, she thought about the enormous amount of time and material needed to produce just one sail. Yet the Danish king Knut II is believed by historians to have had over 1,700 ships in 1085. 'You think about the Vikings' western expansion,' she says. 'And you think, maybe the sheep had something to do with it. And unless there were women ashore making sails, Vikings could never have sailed anywhere.'

Lightfoot's sails have provided some unexpected insights into the handling of Viking ships. For example, woollen sails power Viking ships about ten per cent faster upwind than modern sails, and allow the ships to be sailed far closer to the wind than anyone guessed. In September, the Roskilde museum's latest ship, a reproduction based on the *Skuldelev 2* wreck, is due to make its maiden voyage all the way to Ireland, but despite at least 1,000 years of 'progress', this ship will have to do without a woollen sail. Unlike the Vikings, the museum doesn't have the huge flocks of wild sheep or an army of women to provide the material it needs.

13   What point does the writer make about finding Viking sails?

    A   Written records did not provide any useful information.

    B   Most Viking sails were believed to have been destroyed by fire.

    C   Viking sails had frequently been reused for other purposes.

    D   Archaeologists had not realised where sails might be kept.

14   When Amy Lightfoot was asked to make her first woollen sail, her problem was that

    A   she could obtain no first-hand information about the construction of such sails.

    B   she had to substitute a poorer quality material for Viking sailcloth.

    C   there were no other people in the textile field that she could consult.

    D   the Coastal Museum had unrealistic expectations of who could make it.

15   What are we told about the sail in the third paragraph?

    A   The quality of the cloth depended on the type of boat.

    B   The wool used was taken from one type of sheep.

    C   The wool required the addition of a waterproof substance.

    D   In some ways the cloth used was superior to modern textiles.

16   What are we told about land management in the third paragraph?

    A   Farmers did not appreciate the long-term results of preventing tree growth.

    B   Farmers knew it was essential to encourage the spread of heather.

    C   Disasters such as fire sometimes interfered with land management.

    D   Summer grass became more plentiful because of the sheep.

17   Why did it take Amy Lightfoot so long to make the sail for the *Sara Kjerstine*?

    A   One type of wool she used was of inferior quality.

    B   She had underestimated the number of sheep required.

    C   It was not possible to use modern production methods in the process.

    D   The sail was of a larger size than the one at Trondenes.

18   In the fifth paragraph, what does Amy Lightfoot imply?

    A   The traditional interpretation of Danish history was misleading.

    B   Archaeologists had not appreciated the number of ships the Vikings had.

    C   The amount of time spent on the making of the *Sara Kjerstine* sail was unnecessary.

    D   The role of women in Viking expansion to the west has been overlooked.

19   What point is exemplified by the reference to the Roskilde museum's latest ship?

    A   It is ironic that the museum cannot replicate the same quality cloth that the Vikings had.

    B   It is unlikely that the Vikings would have sailed on the same route to Ireland.

    C   It is possible that the replica ship may succeed where the original failed.

    D   It is surprising that modern sails are not more similar in structure to traditional ones.

Part 4

You are going to read an article about electric guitars. For questions **20–34**, choose from the sections (**A–D**). The sections may be chosen more than once. When more than one answer is required, these may be given **in any order**.

Mark your answers **on the separate answer sheet**.

In which section(s) of the article are the following mentioned?

the advantages to a performer of a particular guitar	20
the fact that to some collectors the instrument itself is more important than who played it	21 22
the fact that music professionals have to compete with others for the most desirable classic guitars	23
the fact that few guitars are sold on the open market	24
how choice was dictated by the tone the make of guitar produced	25
the fact that the most devoted collectors restrict themselves to guitars made during a particular period	26
the fact that where a guitar is discovered is sometimes given importance	27
the way some guitars have been badly treated	28
a guitar which is much more in demand now than when it was first made	29
a particular guitar which is easy to take apart	30
the fact that the guitars of today are very similar to those first produced	31
people having feelings of nostalgia for a certain period in their lives	32
a guitar which unexpectedly appealed to professional musicians	33
a change in the way guitars were made which prompted interest in early instruments	34

Electric Guitars

Eric Clapton's Strat sold for £300,000. Anthony Thorncroft looks at the market which has grown around vintage electric guitars.

A

In the 1960s, electric guitars were everywhere and easily available. They tended, over time, to be laid aside. They were bashed about and raided for parts. This has happened to most old guitars, especially Fenders, which can be swiftly disassembled. But the classics, the early American guitars, are now rare and very collectable, especially if they are in perfect condition.

As a result a global market has grown up around the best guitars. They are often bought by pop stars, but also some computer executives have invested their fortunes made from new technology in this old technology. The sums paid for classic guitars vary enormously, but you might well be asked for £25,000 and rising for a 1954 Fender Stratocaster in perfect original condition.

B

Dealers are keen to add to the mystique of the trade. Unlike other practical objects that have become works of art, notably vintage cars, electric guitars are still mainly traded privately rather than in the glare of the auction room.

Serious collecting of electric guitars began in the 1970s, about the time when manufacturers began to mass-produce inferior instruments. They could no longer afford the right wood. The first electrics had been made mainly from swamp ash and Canadian maple from mature North American forests. So purists collect only the guitars of the 1950s and 1960s.

These things matter to the true believers who know that their passion began around 1948, when Leo Fender introduced what was to become the first commercially available electric guitar – the Fender Broadcaster – in Fullerton, California. It was light, easy to play, gave the musician that essential freedom to shake around on the stage, and was aesthetically pleasing. Fender did the job so well that the basic design of the electric guitar – apart from one-off spectaculars that mainly pandered to the fantasies of individual stars – remains unchanged. By the 1980s, shrewd manufacturers were making copies of these originals.

C

Quite quickly after the Broadcaster came the Telecaster, and then, in 1954, the Stratocaster arrived – the most popular electric guitar of all time. It was designed for the mass market but became the favourite instrument of many rock stars, including Jimi Hendrix. Its main rival was the Gibson Les Paul, which was launched in 1952. If you wanted a light, jangly sound, you went for the Strat; if you preferred it richer and heavier, you favoured Les Paul.

The true collector rather looks down on guitars associated with rock stars, preferring instead a classic Strat or a Gibson Gold Top. He (and they are invariably men) is usually happy with a guitar in Lake Placid Blue or Surf Green, recalling the period when Fender used motor paints.

Over time Gibson experimented, introducing ranges in weird shapes, especially the Flying V of 1958, which proved so unpopular that only 100 were produced, making it rare, and very sought-after with collectors today.

D

Collectors of classic electric guitars are aware of every small variation, every colour change, every mechanical improvement. While many want just one expensive toy, some collectors get hooked and amass a barrage of guitars of different colours and makes. When two fans are locked in an auction battle for a guitar owned by a star, really big money can come into play. The highest price for a guitar bought in a salesroom is the £316,879 paid for the guitar that Eric Clapton used when recording his hit song *Layla*.

But all this is populist hysteria to the true collectors, who are unimpressed by starry associations. They hold early electric guitars in the same reverence with which string players regard the famous violins made by Stradivari. There are even famous old guitars with names reflecting the place where they resurfaced, such as the Basement Burst.

In its time, the electric guitar seemed the fleeting reflection of an age. It has become a symbol of that age and an object of desire for a generation, providing them with access to the long-lost days of their youth.

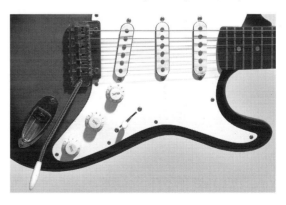

PAPER 2   WRITING (1 hour 30 minutes)

Part 1

You **must** answer this question. Write your answer in **180–220** words in an appropriate style.

---

1   You are studying in Australia and have just completed one week's work experience as an assistant at an activity centre for young people. You now have to write a report for the tutor at your college who organised this work experience.

Read the notice for the activity centre and some extracts from your diary below. Then, **using the information appropriately**, write your report describing your time at the centre, explaining any difficulties you had and saying whether you would recommend the work experience to others.

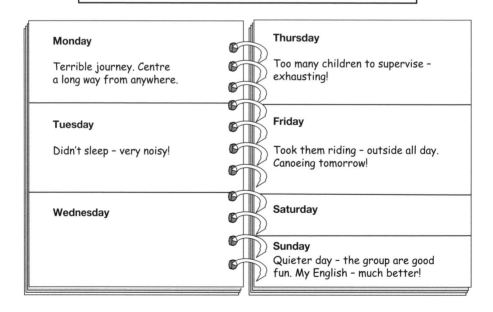

WALTON ACTIVITY CENTRE

Horse riding, canoeing, climbing
Shared accommodation
Lakeside location

Monday

Terrible journey. Centre a long way from anywhere.

Tuesday

Didn't sleep – very noisy!

Wednesday

Thursday

Too many children to supervise – exhausting!

Friday

Took them riding – outside all day. Canoeing tomorrow!

Saturday

Sunday
Quieter day – the group are good fun. My English – much better!

Write your **report**. You should use your own words as far as possible.

Part 2

Write an answer to **one** of the questions **2–5** in this part. Write your answer in **220–260** words in an appropriate style.

---

2   You see the following announcement in an international sports magazine.

> **Good and bad role models**
>
> Today, because of international media coverage, sports people can have a big influence on young people. We would like you to tell us which sports person, in your opinion, is a good role model for young people and who is a bad role model. You should explain why you have chosen these two people. The most interesting replies will win tickets to a sports event of their choice.

Write your **competition entry**.

3   You see this announcement in an international fashion magazine.

> **You are what you wear**
>
> Some people say that you can tell a lot about someone's personality from the clothes they wear. Do you agree? Write an article, telling us what you think and giving your reasons.
>
> We will publish the best articles.

Write your **article**.

4   You see the notice below in an environmental magazine.

> **INTERNATIONAL FUND FOR THE ENVIRONMENT**
>
> The International Fund is awarding grants to develop projects which will have a positive impact on the local environment.
> Write a proposal describing one environmental project you think should be developed and explaining how it would benefit your local community.

Write your **proposal**.

5   Answer **one** of the following two questions based on **one** of the titles below.

(a)   *The Pelican Brief* by John Grisham

You have been asked to write an essay on *The Pelican Brief*. In your essay, explain how Darby Shaw became involved in the case, say whether or not you think she acted foolishly and give reasons for your opinions.

Write your **essay**.

(b)   *Lucky Jim* by Kingsley Amis

You decide to write an article on humour in *Lucky Jim* for a cinema website. In your article, explain how Jim Dixon's bad luck provides a lot of the humour in *Lucky Jim* and say which scene you think is funniest and why.

Write your **article**.

PAPER 3   USE OF ENGLISH (1 hour)

Part 1

For questions **1–12**, read the text below and decide which answer (**A**, **B**, **C** or **D**) best fits each gap. There is an example at the beginning (**0**).

Mark your answers **on the separate answer sheet**.

Example:

0 A known   **B** identified   **C** recognised   **D** acknowledged

0	A	B	C	D
	▬	▢	▢	▢

Dr Seuss

Theodor Seuss Geisel, better **(0)** .... as 'Dr Seuss', began writing for children **(1)** .... by chance. During a long sea voyage in 1936, Seuss amused himself by **(2)** .... together a nonsense poem to the rhythm of the ship's engine. Later he illustrated the rhyme and published it as *And to think that I saw it on Mulberry Street*. Many critics **(3)** .... it as Seuss' best work.

A later book, *McElligot's Pool*, **(4)** .... the first appearance of Seuss' famous fantasy characters, and *Horton Hatches the Egg* introduces an **(5)** .... of morality. Seuss' reputation as a major children's writer was sealed with the publication of *The Cat in the Hat*. This book uses easy-to-read words to tell the story of two children alone at home on a rainy day. A cat wearing a tall hat arrives to entertain them, wrecking their house in the **(6)** .... The enthusiastic **(7)** .... of this book delighted Seuss and **(8)** .... him to found Beginner Books, a publishing company specialising in easy-to-read books for children. Some of his books have been made into cartoons and one of them, *How the Grinch Stole Christmas*, was also made into an ingenious and **(9)** .... successful feature film starring Jim Carrey.

At one point in his career, Seuss **(10)** .... gave up writing for children and **(11)** .... his talents to making documentary films. One of these **(12)** .... a great deal of attention and won an Academy Award.

1   **A** fully   **B** quite   **C** extremely   **D** fairly

2   **A** placing   **B** laying   **C** putting   **D** setting

3   **A** look beyond   **B** look upon   **C** look through   **D** look towards

4   **A** indicates   **B** shows   **C** means   **D** marks

5   **A** amount   **B** ingredient   **C** element   **D** item

6   **A** practice   **B** method   **C** process   **D** action

7   **A** reception   **B** welcome   **C** greeting   **D** admission

8   **A** guided   **B** led   **C** told   **D** pointed

9   **A** highly   **B** intensively   **C** strongly   **D** widely

10 **A** shortly   **B** momentarily   **C** temporarily   **D** presently

11 **A** assigned   **B** allocated   **C** donated   **D** devoted

12 **A** called   **B** attracted   **C** engaged   **D** pulled

Part 2

For questions **13–27**, read the text below and think of the word which best fits each gap. Use only **one** word in each gap. There is an example at the beginning (**0**).

Write your answers **IN CAPITAL LETTERS on the separate answer sheet**.

Example:

0		O	N																

The Mars company

The suburb of McLean (**0**) .... the outskirts of Washington DC may look very ordinary, (**13**) .... it is actually home to the headquarters of the Mars chocolate empire, one of the largest private companies in the US. And yet not (**14**) .... is known about the man who set (**15**) .... some of the most famous chocolate factories in the world. Forrest Mars was a very solitary man, (**16**) .... policy it was never to give an interview. His son, Forrest Junior, who took over the running of the company when his father died, seems to share the same obsession (**17**) .... secrecy. He refuses to address the workforce and has not been photographed since (**18**) .... days at college. He (**19**) .... even said to wear disguises (**20**) .... conducting business with outsiders.

The Mars company is run on rules which seem to come from an earlier era. All employees, from the top of the company to the bottom, receive an annual 10% bonus (**21**) .... arriving at work on time throughout the year. Everyone is treated equally. All Mars managers – Forrest Junior included – must do (**22**) .... own photocopying and are not allowed to travel first class.

(**23**) .... modern standards, the company operates with an amazing lack of bureaucracy. In fact, it is completely (**24**) .... company policy to write memos, and meetings can (**25**) .... take place when there is something (**26**) .... importance to discuss. Elaborate presentations are considered a waste of time. Yet (**27**) .... is perhaps these tight systems that have in part helped to make Mars a successful international company.

Part 3

For questions **28–37**, read the text below. Use the word given in capitals at the end of some of the lines to form a word that fits in the gap **in the same line**. There is an example at the beginning (**0**).

Write your answers **IN CAPITAL LETTERS on the separate answer sheet**.

Example:

0	D	E	V	E	L	O	P	E	R	S						

Ecological consultants

Ecological consultants are hired to advise **(0)** .... in the construction
industry on the impact their work may have on protected wildlife. Their
(28) .... role is to prevent the client from getting into trouble with
environmental laws by advising on habitats, obtaining permits and **(29)** ....
the negative effects on the countryside of the proposed development.

DEVELOP

PRIME

MINIMUM

In order to do this work **(30)** .... , a deep knowledge and love of nature is
essential, as is a **(31)** .... to work in outdoor conditions that are sometimes
uncomfortable. A head for business and excellent presentation skills are
also necessary for the job. Consultants have to be **(32)** .... to clients'
needs while at the same time ensuring government regulations are followed.
So the ability to assimilate data from a variety of sources is **(33)** ....

EFFECT

WILLING

SYMPATHY

DISPENSE

To become an ecological consultant, a **(34)** .... in ecology, planning or
land management may be required. However, **(35)** .... experience is also
important as **(36)** .... for jobs is fierce.

QUALIFY

PRACTISE

COMPETE

Young people interested in a career as an ecological consultant can gain
(37) .... with a range of relevant techniques by doing voluntary work with
a conservation organisation in their area.

FAMILIAR

Part 4

For questions **38–42**, think of **one** word only which can be used appropriately in all three sentences. Here is an example (**0**).

Example:

0 They say the new minister is a lovely person and very .... to talk to.

My neighbours have not had a very .... life, but they always seem cheerful.

It's .... enough to see why the town is popular with tourists.

Example:

| **0** | E | A | S | Y | | | | | | | | | | | |

Write **only** the missing word **IN CAPITAL LETTERS on the separate answer sheet.**

---

38   By the age of five, children have a good .... of right and wrong.

In dogs, the .... of hearing is very highly developed.

It is not obvious to me in what .... this word is being used.

39   In class today, our chemistry teacher gave us very .... instructions about how we should proceed with the experiment.

It was .... to everyone watching that the athlete had not recovered from his injury.

The water is very .... on this side of the bay and you can see plenty of fish.

40   My heart .... when I realised we had to walk another ten kilometres before we got to the youth hostel.

The ship .... without trace over three hundred years ago.

We were out playing with the children when the neighbours' dog .... its teeth into the ball and ran off with it.

41   Once you hear her .... of the story, I'm sure you'll understand why she resigned.

I could see Chen on the far .... of the room, talking to the Russian delegates.

Our .... lost 2–1 in Saturday's match and that knocks them out of the cup.

42   Chris Cummings was a good guitarist but he couldn't be trusted to .... up on time for concerts, so the band asked him to leave.

At Open Days, the second-year students .... potential students and their parents round all the facilities.

He's an excellent diver but when he's on the diving board in front of an audience he has an unfortunate tendency to .... off.

Part 5

For questions **43–50**, complete the second sentence so that it has a similar meaning to the first sentence, using the word given. **Do not change the word given.** You must use between **three** and **six** words, including the word given. Here is an example (**0**).

Example:

0 James would only speak to the head of department alone.

ON

James .... to the head of department alone.

The gap can be filled with the words 'insisted on speaking', so you write:

Example: | **0** | INSISTED ON SPEAKING

Write **only** the missing words **IN CAPITAL LETTERS on the separate answer sheet.**

---

43 Flooding after a heavy storm was responsible for the damage to the bridge.

CAUSED

The damage to the bridge .... after a heavy storm.

44 When we arrive isn't really important, as long as we get there.

MATTER

It really .... time we arrive, as long as we get there.

45 I want to buy a car but, without your financial help, I'll be unable to do it.

ABLE

I want to buy a car but I won't .... you help me financially.

46   It was impossible to predict all the problems that we faced when we built our own house.

PREDICTED

Nobody could .... face so many problems when we built our own house.

47   Gail wished she had followed David's suggestions about preparing for the interview.

DOING

Gail regretted .... about preparing for the interview.

48   After a sleepless night, Marta finally decided that she wouldn't accept the job she had been offered.

MIND

After a sleepless night, Marta finally .... accept the job she had been offered.

49   Although Joe kept on attempting to contact his cousin, he didn't manage to speak to her until the next day.

TOUCH

Despite repeated .... his cousin, Joe didn't manage to speak to her until the next day.

50   The huge traffic jam on the motorway delayed us for several hours.

HELD

The huge traffic jam on the motorway .... for several hours.

PAPER 4   LISTENING (approximately 40 minutes)

Part 1

You will hear three different extracts. For questions **1–6**, choose the answer (**A**, **B** or **C**) which fits best according to what you hear. There are two questions for each extract.

Extract One

You overhear two people talking at a party about a round-the-world trip.

1   Why did the man decide not to take his car?

    A   It could have ruled out certain destinations.

    B   He was concerned about the environmental impact.

    C   People thought it was an unimaginative way to travel.

2   When looking back on his trip, the man is

    A   pointing out the long-term benefits.

    B   suggesting possible areas to visit.

    C   outlining the potential risks.

Extract Two

You hear part of an interview with a sculptor.

3   What made him create the figure of a horse and its rider?

    A   the strong liking which he has for animals

    B   the fact that the horse had become very well known

    C   the strength of the owner's feelings about the horse

4   His advice for aspiring artists is

    A   to remain true to oneself.

    B   to study the work of others.

    C   to avoid losing confidence if work is rejected.

Extract Three

You hear part of an interview with Carol Mills, who recently completed a 700-kilometre sledge race from Canada to the North Pole.

5   Carol thinks her achievements on the trip were a result of

    A her leadership training.

    B her ability to work in a team.

    C her skill at taking care of herself.

6   How has the trip changed Carol's attitude to work?

    A She's more ambitious about her career.

    B She's no longer scared of new challenges.

    C She's more determined to solve people's difficulties.

Part 2

You will hear a talk about Hugh Munro, an important figure in the history of mountain climbing in Scotland. For questions **7–14**, complete the sentences.

HUGH MUNRO AND MOUNTAIN CLIMBING IN SCOTLAND

Hugh Munro was asked to provide a

	7

of the highest mountains in Scotland.

The mountain areas had previously been used mostly for

	8

and cattle farming.

In the nineteenth century, road and rail links to the Highlands were developed and

	9

were produced.

In the 1930s, the growth of leisure activities such as hiking and

	10

gave more access to mountain areas.

In the 1930s, unemployed people from the shipbuilding and

	11

industries took up climbing.

Some people who were short of money had to use

	12

to get to the mountains.

Today, the challenge of climbing all Munro's mountains is known as

'	13

the Munros' by climbers.

The speaker uses the phrase

	14

to describe the recent

popularity of climbing Munro's mountains.

Visual materials for the Speaking test

- What difficulties might the photographers be having?
- Who might be interested in the photographs they are taking?

- How might the people be feeling?
- What might have caused them to feel like this?

- What hopes and fears for the future might each chapter include?
- Which chapter might interest readers most?

- Why might the people have chosen to communicate in these ways?
- How difficult might it be for them to communicate effectively?

- Why might the people be working in conditions like these?
- What problems might they have?

- Why might children remember experiences like these?
- Which two experiences would have the greatest influence on children's lives?

- Why might the people have chosen to be in these situations?
- How might the people be feeling?

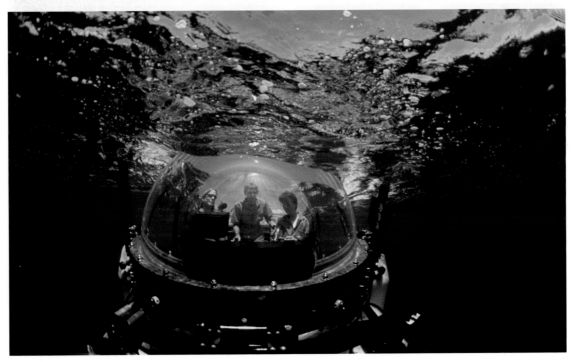

- What might the atmosphere in these places be like?
- How might the audiences react to the music?

- What might be the advantages and disadvantages of taking up these careers?
- Which one would provide the best long-term career prospects?

Visual materials for the Speaking test

- What might the people be talking about?
- How might the listeners be feeling?

- How are the people using their senses?
- What might happen as a result?

- What messages are these advertisements trying to communicate?
- Which advertisement would be the most successful in persuading people to buy the product?

Part 3

You will hear a radio interview with a young novelist called Nic Farren, who is talking about his writing and his experience of working in bookshops. For questions **15–20**, choose the answer (**A**, **B**, **C** or **D**) which fits best according to what you hear.

---

15 Nic says that while trying to write his novel and study at the same time, he became

    A determined to do both well.
    B resentful of the demands of his course.
    C tempted to simply copy other writers' work.
    D worried about the need to do research for his writing.

16 When asked about his writer's notebook, Nic says he was

    A restricted by the lack of space for illustrations.
    B keen to record his moments of creativity.
    C fascinated by the different directions it took him in.
    D put off by the thought of others reading it.

17 How does Nic feel about the prospect of seeing his own book on sale where he works?

    A worried about seeing copies returned unsold to the publisher
    B apprehensive about hearing his colleagues' opinion of it
    C sure he'll mention to customers that he's the author
    D relieved that it will finally be available to buy

18 What does Nic find attractive about working in a bookshop?

    A the opportunity to talk to people who share his tastes
    B having the chance to indulge his passion for reading
    C the quiet atmosphere he gets to work in
    D being surrounded by great literature

19 Nic thinks customers liked the first bookshop he worked in because

    A they were allowed to use staff facilities if they wished.
    B the owner was keen to get them what they wanted.
    C it was in a very pleasant location.
    D they were under no pressure to buy.

20 Nic suspects that the typical image of a bookseller is of someone who

    A is generally bad-tempered.
    B is indifferent to customers' needs.
    C is too interested in their own opinions.
    D isn't knowledgeable about their product.

Part 4

You will hear five short extracts in which people are talking about awards they have received in recognition of achievements in their working lives.

TASK ONE

For questions **21–25**, choose from the list (**A–H**) what each person's achievement was.

TASK TWO

For questions **26–30**, choose from the list (**A–H**) the result of each person's achievement.

While you listen you must complete both tasks.

A an act of courage			**A** better working conditions being introduced		
B exceptional loyalty	Speaker 1	21	**B** new software being used	Speaker 1	26
C showing originality	Speaker 2	22	**C** greater self-confidence	Speaker 2	27
D cutting back on expenditure	Speaker 3	23	**D** a technological revolution	Speaker 3	28
E managerial competence	Speaker 4	24	**E** a potential disaster being avoided	Speaker 4	29
F gaining a formal qualification	Speaker 5	25	**F** an increase in turnover	Speaker 5	30
G winning a competition			**G** the right staff being recruited		
H long-term service			**H** people being looked after properly		

PAPER 5   SPEAKING (15 minutes)

There are two examiners. One (the interlocutor) conducts the test, providing you with the necessary materials and explaining what you have to do. The other examiner (the assessor) is introduced to you, but then takes no further part in the interaction.

Part 1 (3 minutes)

The interlocutor first asks you and your partner a few questions. The interlocutor asks candidates for some information about themselves, then widens the scope of the questions by asking about e.g. candidates' leisure activities, studies, travel and daily life. Candidates are expected to respond to the interlocutor's questions and listen to what their partner has to say.

Part 2 (a one-minute 'long turn' for each candidate, plus a 30-second response from the second candidate)

You are each given the opportunity to talk for about a minute, and to comment briefly after your partner has spoken.

The interlocutor gives you a set of pictures and asks you to talk about them for about one minute. It is important to listen carefully to the interlocutor's instructions. The interlocutor then asks your partner a question about your pictures and your partner responds briefly.

You are then given another set of pictures to look at. Your partner talks about these pictures for about one minute. This time the interlocutor asks you a question about your partner's pictures and you respond briefly.

Part 3 (approximately 4 minutes)

In this part of the test you and your partner are asked to talk together. The interlocutor places a new set of pictures on the table between you. This stimulus provides the basis for a discussion. The interlocutor explains what you have to do.

Part 4 (approximately 4 minutes)

The interlocutor asks some further questions, which leads to a more general discussion of what you have talked about in Part 3. You may comment on your partner's answers if you wish.

Test 4

PAPER 1 READING (1 hour 15 minutes)

Part 1

You are going to read three extracts which are all concerned in some way with the natural world. For questions **1–6**, choose the answer (**A**, **B**, **C** or **D**) which you think fits best according to the text. Mark your answers **on the separate answer sheet**.

Camping in the wild

We live in an age when the world's wild areas are becoming increasingly accessible. Being able to visit fantastic natural sights before retreating to the warmth and comfort of a centrally heated hotel has become almost commonplace: national parks such as Torres del Paine in Chile offer luxury accommodation. But wrapping yourself in air-conditioned sumptuousness serves only to insulate you from the very environment that you've come to experience. Even staying on an organised campsite is still a step away from experiencing nature in the raw. And that is where wilderness camping comes in.

The first thing to appreciate is the level of responsibility that comes with the privilege of camping in the wild. Every tent peg stabbed in the ground, every groundsheet laid out and every stove fire has the potential to scar the landscape. Take for example the seemingly innocuous act of picking up large rocks to place on tent anchors around your tent. Ignoring for a moment the habitat destruction caused by moving boulders, picture the dismay on the faces of the next posse of backpackers to come across the same *line 13* beautiful spot, only to discover the tell-tale circle of stones. Second-hand wilderness camping is never as memorable as the illusion of being the first to camp in a special place. So if you remember that every action has a consequence, and if you are able to think through every stage of wild camping, you'll have a better time of it, the surrounding terrain will suffer less damage and future campers will appreciate your thoughtfulness.

1 What point is the writer making in the first paragraph?

  A It is a shame that national parks only offer luxury accommodation.
  B Camping in the wild can offer a unique experience.
  C It isn't necessary to be uncomfortable to make the most of wild areas.
  D Tourists are increasingly keen to try camping in the wild.

2 What would the backpackers referred to in line 13 be dismayed by?

  A the amount of responsibility they have for the environment
  B the realisation that other campers had different attitudes
  C the destruction of the local environment
  D the physical evidence of previous camping

Extract from a novel

THE BIG STORM

The storm went on all night long and into the middle of the morning, an extraordinary affair. I have never known the like for violence or duration. I was sitting up in bed, the light flickering around me and the sky stamping up and down in fury, breaking its bones. At last, I thought, at last the elements have achieved a pitch of magnificence to match my inner turmoil! In this mood of euphoria I considered my position in a new light.

I have always had the conviction, resistant to all rational considerations, that at some unspecified future moment, the continuous rehearsal which has been my life until now, with its many misreadings, its twists and turns, will be done with and that the real drama for which I have been preparing with such earnestness will at last begin. *line 10* It is a common delusion, I know; everyone entertains it. Yet last night, in the midst of the spectacular display, I wondered if the moment of my entrance might be imminent, the moment of my *going on*, so to say. I do not know how it would be, this dramatic leap into the thick of the action, or what exactly might be expected to take place, on stage. But what I am looking forward to is a moment of expression. I shall be totally fulfilled. I shall be delivered, like a noble closing speech.

3   Which of the following sums up the writer's response to the storm?

   A   He was angry that it kept him awake.
   B   It made him feel inadequate.
   C   It reflected his own emotions.
   D   He was frightened by its intensity.

4   What does the writer explain about his intuition that the 'real drama' of his life is about to begin (*line 10*)?

   A   It allows him to accept his past mistakes.
   B   It is a sensation that few others share.
   C   It is something he has always been ready for.
   D   It is based on a rational analysis of events.

PROTECTING THE GREAT BARRIER REEF

The Great Barrier Reef stretches along the Queensland coastline in Australia. Historically, it has been regarded as a well-protected, pristine wonderland – a haven of delicate corals and abundant fish. Yet as scientists came to understand more about the reef's complexities, a different picture emerged. Overfishing, land-based pollution and coral bleaching, exacerbated by increased sea temperatures due to global warming, were all impacting on its natural wealth.

Immediate action was required because, contrary to popular belief, only 4.6% of the reef was fully protected. As a result of public campaigning, the Australian government committed to a plan to protect 33% of the reef, with the Great Barrier Reef Marine Park zoning plan being implemented in 2004. This is the world's largest network of marine sanctuaries, covering over 11 million hectares.

Yet the reef is still under threat. The amount of sediment flowing from the land into the marine park from its catchment area has quadrupled over the past 150 years, due largely to grazing and cropping expansion and loss of native vegetation and wetlands. The reef has experienced two mass coral bleaching events in 1998 and 2002, when the corals lost colour due to an increase in water temperature. And finally, not only is the reef subject to high levels of fishing pressure, but other fishing practices, such as sea-floor trawling of prawns, are still permitted in over half of the marine park, resulting in untargeted fish capture and destruction of the sea floor.

5 What misconception existed about the Great Barrier Reef in the past?

  A It would not be adversely affected by global warming.
  B It possessed marine life not found elsewhere.
  C It was safeguarded for future generations.
  D It was the largest reef in the world.

6 According to the text, what problem is being caused by a legal commercial activity?

  A coral bleaching
  B destruction of the sea floor
  C pollution of the wetlands
  D increased sea temperatures

Part 2

You are going to read an extract from a magazine article. Six paragraphs have been removed from the extract. Choose from the paragraphs **A–G** the one which fits each gap (**7–12**). There is one extra paragraph which you do not need to use. Mark your answers **on the separate answer sheet**.

Elephant Intelligence

Should elephants be moved to near the top of the animal intelligence list?

For the first time, remote-control cameras have infiltrated the elephant herds of Africa. The result has been made into a documentary film shown in many countries around the world. On watching the footage, you start to believe that elephants may indeed be as intelligent as the great apes. As film-maker John Downer says, 'When you see the immense co-operation and sensitivity between these animals, you realise that they must be extremely clever.'

7	

'This communication and understanding is impressive,' says Downer. 'I know of no other species, apart from ourselves, who gather to greet a newborn.' Iain Douglas-Hamilton, chairman of the organisation Save the Elephants, voices similar sentiments. 'The behaviour suggests that the same emotions exist between one elephant and another as exist between humans. I believe elephants, like ourselves, have a sense of humour, of play and of mischievousness.'

8	

So what evidence for elephant intelligence can be found? Self-awareness is a key ability of conscious beings. And just as a person looking into their mirror and seeing a dirty face will try to wipe it, it has been found that an elephant studying its reflection will try to rub smudges off its forehead with its trunk.

9	

The same might be said of the way in which elephants choose to gather in particular groups of different sizes and at different times. Sometimes they are in an intimate family group, at other times they join other families to make a bond group. For a long time it was a mystery as to how these groups co-ordinated themselves.

10	

Cameraman Michael Roberts noticed this: 'I recorded elephants freezing for long periods, their trunks close to the ground, listening to things the human ear could not detect. But perhaps the most amazing thing was seeing them using sticks to remove flies from their bodies. Imagine that – elephants actually using tools, and, what's more, passing down their skills to their young.'

11	

Iain Douglas-Hamilton is convinced that elephants plan their moves between 'safe areas', sprinting from one protected reserve to another under cover of darkness, and avoiding the danger areas in between. 'How the elephants can tell the two apart is unclear,' he says. 'It's not as if there are any fences. And it's unlikely that any single elephant's experience of encounters with hunters would be extensive enough to equip it with an accurate mental map of protected reserve boundaries.'

12

But this store of social knowledge may be at risk. Families with older matriarchs tend to have healthier babies. Unfortunately, the oldest individuals are also the largest, and these tend to be prime targets for hunters. If groups rely on these individuals for social knowledge, then a whole family's survival may be affected by the removal of a few key individuals.

A The footage from the cameras gives us an answer, backing up the theory that elephants communicate through seismic-evoking sounds that are transmitted through the earth, like mini earthquakes. These allow the elephants to assess where they are in relation to one another and to alert others to their physical or emotional state.

B So however clever elephants are, they are still at the mercy of humans, who have been the perpetrators of most of the species' problems of survival. With evidence mounting of elephant intelligence and wide-ranging communication between one another, there is a need for a rise in their status on the intelligence spectrum.

C For example, they have the capacity to appreciate the needs of others. At one point a group of female elephants gathers around a baby elephant. The baby is struggling to get to his feet, and all the females get involved in trying to help him up. When a male arrives and tries to interfere, female reinforcements are quickly called in to prevent him from trampling the baby.

D If individuals cannot acquire sufficient knowledge, this suggests that the animals may also be learning from the experiences of others. 'The precision with which they act,' he continues, 'suggests their exchange of information is more sophisticated than anyone had previously believed.'

E This discovery, when it occurred some years ago, was a startling one for scientists, who had assumed that only humans and higher apes were smart enough to achieve self-recognition. Many behavioural researchers consider that ability to be a hallmark of complex intelligence.

F Learning what to fear is also acquired from their elders. In the Amboseli region, where Masai tribesmen occasionally hunt elephants, the elephants learn to run from the sight and smell of the Masai. Even tapes of Masai voices will cause the elephants to flee, while they ignore the sight, smell and sound of tourists.

G Similarities are also evident in the tendency of elephants to be jealous and crochety, as shown in the shot of a female lashing out with her back foot to kick a troublesome young elephant.

Part 3

You are going to read a newspaper article. For questions **13–19**, choose the answer (**A**, **B**, **C** or **D**) which you think fits best according to the text. Mark your answers **on the separate answer sheet**.

The Sound of Music

Geoff Brown wonders whether film music can ever be regarded as art.

No one can claim such mastery of the fantasy blockbuster sound as British film-music composer John Williams. It's a style of music he did much to define in *Star Wars* and then for many other films for the director Steven Spielberg. There are distinctive melodies which give the feeling of flying, snatches of music to represent different characters, and intricate illustrative details. In addition, everything follows the symphonic style of a hundred years ago. It's what the film industry in Hollywood wants, it's what John Williams supplies, and what audiences everywhere expect.

Can we call it art, or is it simply an interesting artefact, a sort of factory product? For the cinema-goer sitting with a popcorn bag the question doesn't arise. But since film music now spreads to a different audience far outside cinemas, on lavishly promoted soundtrack CDs and serious concert platforms, it may be interesting to answer the question.

Composers themselves have expressed very diverse opinions. Interviewed some years ago, Williams himself proudly referred to film music as 'the opera of the 20th century'. On the other hand, Richard Rodney Bennett, the composer of the music for the film *Murder on the Orient Express*, declared that 'in writing film music one is really using only a sixth of one's musical mind'. Everyone agrees on one point though: the rewards are pleasingly high. There are royalties. And if you hit the right buttons you can spin off into the lucrative sideline of a concert career, regularly mounting live performances of film compositions.

But if you consider the working conditions that composers put up with, superficially the odds do seem stacked against film music being classed as art. First of all, film music is composed in snippets, timed to the second, and written after the film is shot. Then there are insane deadlines – like having five days to compose 50 minutes of music. Next, the composer has to live with the fact that he/she wields no artistic control. Finally, the ultimate insult is that what is written struggles to get itself noticed against a background of dialogue, squeals, and every possible visual delight from cartoon character *Shrek's* green body to actor Tom Cruise's chin. It can't be art, can it?

But think of the German composer Bach in the eighteenth century, satisfying his employers by writing one cantata a week. Few composers can write without a commission. And for the true artist, rules and restrictions stimulate. Film scoring can sharpen a composer's technique, encourage experimentation. The composer Vaughan Williams was never quite the same again after his work on the film *Scott of the Antarctic* caused him to branch into percussion instruments as a way of capturing a frozen landscape.

Film music can be art then, and has been, in fits and starts. The frustrating thing is that many film producers have limited expectations of what film music can be. Once the age of silent movies was over and talkies arrived, music became an integral part of the projected film and anything was possible. Music didn't have to be poured over the images like mayonnaise; it could argue with them, puncture them with irony, or rudely interrupt. In Europe, various composers such as Shostakovich and Hanns Eisler experimented with timbre and form, showing Hollywood (at the time still stuck with the sounds of a late nineteenth-century symphony orchestra beavering away) that innovative techniques were possible.

But even in Hollywood, art raised its head. All film composers look up to Bernard Herrmann, a giant who coloured each score with a different sound and let his music snake through the images in unconventional ways. The power of the film *Vertigo* lies not only in the director's images but in Herrmann's worried woodwind and turbulent strings and the weird harp solos that dog the characters' footsteps. His scores are usually so interwoven with their films that it's a futile task trying to carve the music into selections for concert use. Herrmann proves that it's even possible to write film scores in bulk without hurtling into an artistic decline.

So, what's my conclusion? Art or factory product? Both in fact, although there's rather more of the factory product than I would like at times.

13   What point is the writer making about John Williams' music in the first paragraph?

   A   It is similar to that produced by other composers.
   B   It is too old-fashioned to remain popular for long.
   C   It has a better reputation in Hollywood than elsewhere.
   D   It has certain characteristics that are easy to identify.

14   In the second paragraph, what does the writer imply about the attitude of cinema-goers to film music?

   A   They are only interested in it if they can purchase the CD.
   B   They perceive it as being mass-produced.
   C   They are not concerned about whether it has artistic merit.
   D   They feel music is an important part of the cinema experience.

15   According to the writer, which view of film music do all composers share?

   A   They consider that it is a worthy outlet for their talents.
   B   They appreciate the financial gains they make from it.
   C   They need it to supplement their main source of income.
   D   They can use it as a way into an alternative career.

16   According to the writer, what is the worst aspect of a film composer's working conditions?

   A   The music has to be composed after the film is completed.
   B   The deadlines set for the composer cannot be achieved.
   C   The music has to compete for attention with other elements of the film.
   D   The composer has no control over how the music is used.

17   The writer compares modern film composers with Bach to show that

   A   some composers work better under pressure.
   B   composers have unreasonable demands imposed on them.
   C   composers must aim to please their employers.
   D   all composers need some sort of sponsorship.

18   What point is made about Hollywood film music when the 'talkies' arrived?

   A   It used less well-known symphony orchestras than before.
   B   It did not constitute a major part of the final production.
   C   It didn't generally make use of new ideas.
   D   It was not considered to make an artistic contribution to the film.

19   What does the writer say is special about Bernard Herrmann's music?

   A   It is of high quality because he composed very little.
   B   It has a distinctive style which evokes the animal world.
   C   It is totally integrated with the visual element of the film.
   D   It has considerable potential for concert performance.

Part 4

You are going to read a magazine article about keeping a journal. For questions **20–34**, choose from the sections (**A–E**). The sections may be chosen more than once. When more than one answer is required, these may be given **in any order**.

Mark your answers **on the separate answer sheet**.

In which section(s) is the following mentioned?

the reader's advantage in knowing an event's later significance	**20** ☐
the journal-writer's desire to tell the truth	**21** ☐
the difference in the writer's perspective between journals and other literary forms	**22** ☐
the vivid recreation of a sensory experience	**23** ☐
the journal as a record of the changes a person undergoes during his or her life	**24** ☐
the unique nature of each person's journal	**25** ☐
the journal-writer's compulsion to make his or her mark on the world	**26** ☐
the primary intended readership of the journal	**27** ☐
the similarity between the journal's narrative and the course of real life	**28** ☐
the journal-writer using the journal as a means of self-criticism	**29** ☐
the relative lack of skill needed for journal-writing	**30** ☐
the writing of an imaginary journal	**31** ☐
the fact that journal-writing is not evaluated in the same way as other literary forms	**32** ☐
the fact that the journal-writer cannot foretell how events and situations will develop	**33** ☐ **34** ☐

KEEPING A JOURNAL

What makes the day-by-day account of a person's life and thoughts so appealing and enduring? William Boyd examines this unique literary form.

A

There are many sorts of journals: journals recording banal details of ordinary lives, and journals intended to witness momentous events. There are others designed simply as an aid to memory, perhaps a rough draft for writing a later, more polished work. But within these varying ambitions and motivations is a common factor uniting all these endeavours – the aspiration to be honest. The implication is that in the privacy of this personal record, things will be uncensored, things will be said that couldn't or wouldn't be uttered in a more public forum. But there is also perhaps a more fundamental drive to our journal-keeping; we want to leave a trace of some kind. Like the adolescent who carves his name on a tree, the act of writing seems to say: I was here.

B

Re-reading the journal I'd kept between 19 and 21 was a disturbing experience. The factual account I would give now of those years would be essentially the same, but the psychological content seems to belong to someone else. There was also a kind of pitiless self-examination of almost everything I did that I cannot remember undertaking. And I was very hard on myself, often insulting myself ruthlessly in the second person. Clearly, I had been much unhappier then than I had thought. But the hard evidence of my journal is irrefutable. However, this schism between my memory of my earlier self and the historical facts made me wonder if the journal served another, more covert purpose for its keeper, namely to chart the various stages of our life. We do become transformed as people and even though our fundamental natures may remain the same, our memories will play us false about our past.

C

This thesis was put into practice when I decided to write my novel *Any Human Heart* as the fictional intimate journal of a fictional writer. It was a paradoxical exercise because in writing it, I had to remain true to another constant that is a defining feature of the journal form. For the journal – relating as it does a life-story – does so in a manifestly different manner from the other forms available, whether biography, memoir or autobiography. All these are fashioned by looking backwards, informed by hindsight, and the impenetrable judgements of

the future often undermine the honest analysis of the present. Only the journal really reflects the day-by-day progress of life. Events have not yet acquired their retrospective significance; for instance the job you were so excited about has still to turn tedious. The journal has to have the same random shape as a human life because it's governed by chance. In essence, it mimics and reflects our own wayward passage through time like no other form of writing.

D

However apparently unimportant the entries, the journal offers us a special insight into the author's life. On occasion, we are provided with a privileged knowledge of their destiny. Scotsman James Boswell – later close friend and biographer of the writer Dr Johnson – writes on 16 May 1763: *'I drank tea at Mr Davies's, and about seven came in the great Mr Samuel Johnson, whom I have so long wished to see . . . As I knew his mortal antipathy to the Scotch, I cried to Davies, "Don't tell him where I come from!"'* As he describes his first sight of the great literary man we participate in his excitement, but there's an extra thrill delivered by our foreknowledge of their later friendship. Often, however, we read with the same ignorance as that of the journal-keeper as he writes. On 21 September 1870, the English diarist Francis Kilvert describes a visit to an orchard and notes: *'The smell of the apples very strong.'* This bears a kind of witness to 21 September 1870 that has as cogent and undeniable validity as any other.

E

Which brings me to the final characteristic of journal-keeping: although we might hope that others may read our observations one distant day, the intimate journal is principally designed to be read by only one pair of eyes: the author's. It is therefore judged by standards of integrity, honesty and immediacy that require no special education, talent or gift. Poetry, the novel, biography and journalism are weighed up by different criteria. Not everyone can write a novel, but everyone is, in theory, capable of keeping a journal. And if you do keep one, then it becomes, in a real sense, the book of your life and a document like no other that has ever been written. But there is also a universality to journal-writing. An intimate journal – if it is true and honest – will also speak to everyone who has a chance to read it.

PAPER 2   WRITING (1 hour 30 minutes)

Part 1

You **must** answer this question. Write your answer in **180–220** words in an appropriate style.

1   Last summer you went on a residential English course at a language school in the UK. Your friend Jan has written to you asking about it.

Read the extract from Jan's letter and from your diary below. Then, **using the information appropriately**, write a letter to Jan describing your experience, saying whether or not you would recommend the residential English course, giving reasons for your opinions.

> Do you think I'd like the course? I've studied lots of grammar – I really need lots of speaking practice. I'd like to do some sightseeing while I'm in the UK too, but I hope there aren't any hidden costs!
>
> Jan

Aug 4
Friendly people and great location – accessible and shops handy.

Aug 12
2 hrs grammar – not again! Useful conversation classes.

Aug 17
Oxford visit – interesting – not cheap and not inc. in course fees!

Aug 24
London trip – wow! Great museums (free!) – but not all students spoke English – annoying!!

Write your **letter**. You should use your own words as far as possible. You do not need to include postal addresses.

Part 2

Write an answer to **one** of the questions **2–5** in this part. Write your answer in **220–260** words in an appropriate style.

---

2   In class, you have been discussing what makes a successful international music star. Your teacher has asked you to write an essay on the following topic:

How much is international success as a music star due to image and good marketing rather than the music?

Write your **essay**.

3   You see the following announcement in a magazine.

> ### Your Best Friend
> We are going to produce a special edition on friendship. We would like you, our readers, to tell us about your best friend. We want to know what you think the most important characteristics of your friend are, what important lessons you have learned from your friend and whether or not you think your friendship will change.

Write your **article**.

4   You see this announcement in a TV magazine.

> ## KTV Productions
> Some reality TV programmes are 'real-life documentaries', which film ordinary people's daily lives. Others are 'reality game shows', which film people attempting various difficult tasks. We produce both types of programme and are interested in viewers' opinions. Please write us a report briefly describing one reality show of each type you have watched, explaining which show you found more entertaining and saying whether you would consider participating in a reality show.

Write your **report**.

5   Answer **one** of the following two questions based on **one** of the titles below.

(a)   *Lucky Jim* by Kingsley Amis

Your teacher has asked you to write an essay on two of the characters in *Lucky Jim.* In your essay, compare the characters of Jim Dixon and Professor Welch and say who you feel more sympathetic towards and why.

Write your **essay**.

(b)   *The Pelican Brief* by John Grisham

You decide to write an article on *The Pelican Brief* for a cinema website. In your article, say which **two** events from the story are the most visual and give reasons for your opinions.

Write your **article**.

PAPER 3   USE OF ENGLISH (1 hour)

Part 1

For questions **1–12**, read the text below and decide which answer (**A**, **B**, **C** or **D**) best fits each gap. There is an example at the beginning (**0**).

Mark your answers **on the separate answer sheet**.

Example:

0 A firmly   **B** strictly   **C** steadily   **D** tightly

0	A	B	C	D
	▬	▭	▭	▭

Shoe Museum

Sonja Bata, the chairwoman of Toronto's Shoe Museum, **(0)** .... believes that footwear speaks a global language. At the Shoe Museum, there are some 10,000 boots and shoes on display, **(1)** .... from Egyptian tomb shoes dating from 2,500 BC to shoes **(2)** .... by pop stars like Madonna. 'The more I **(3)** .... the subject,' says Sonja, 'the more I find that footwear **(4)** .... more about the world of the wearer than any other article of clothing. Shoes give you a real **(5)** .... into their owners' lives.'

Sonja has been obsessed with shoes and their importance in social history since she **(6)** .... a sandal with a very interesting shape in a market in India. She discovered that, for religious reasons, the central platform of the sandal was raised to avoid **(7)** .... insects.

This discovery encouraged Sonja to gather shoes from dozens of countries to find out more about what **(8)** .... behind their design. 'Take the Canadian moccasin shoe,' she says. 'At first **(9)** .... , the design seemed to me completely **(10)** .... because a moccasin is soft and easily worn down by outdoor life. I just couldn't **(11)** .... why it was like that. But then I found that, when they went hunting, the Canadians had to **(12)** .... up quietly on animals – so it is a perfectly designed shoe for this purpose.'

This, and many other fascinating facts, can be learnt on a visit to the Toronto Shoe Museum.

1	**A**	ranking	**B**	running	**C**	ranging	**D**	reaching
2	**A**	awarded	**B**	granted	**C**	offered	**D**	donated
3	**A**	look through	**B**	look into	**C**	look up	**D**	look over
4	**A**	reveals	**B**	exhibits	**C**	presents	**D**	describes
5	**A**	comprehension	**B**	feeling	**C**	insight	**D**	opinion
6	**A**	remarked	**B**	spotted	**C**	regarded	**D**	distinguished
7	**A**	splitting	**B**	grinding	**C**	squeezing	**D**	crushing
8	**A**	hung	**B**	attached	**C**	lay	**D**	rested
9	**A**	glance	**B**	glimpse	**C**	gaze	**D**	glare
10	**A**	unreasonable	**B**	illogical	**C**	incorrect	**D**	unjust
11	**A**	pick up	**B**	take on	**C**	get over	**D**	make out
12	**A**	step	**B**	glide	**C**	slip	**D**	creep

Part 2

For questions **13–27**, read the text below and think of the word which best fits each gap. Use only **one** word in each gap. There is an example at the beginning (**0**).

Write your answers **IN CAPITAL LETTERS on the separate answer sheet.**

Example: | **0** | H | A | S | | | | | | | | | | | | | | | |

Exploring the Arctic Ocean

A huge international project to explore the Arctic Ocean **(0)** .... begun. It is expected to discover thousands of new species of marine animals, many of **(13)** .... have been completely cut **(14)** .... from the rest of the world for thousands of years. Scientists claim that the study of the unknown depths of the Arctic Ocean, perhaps the **(15)** .... understood ocean on earth, is now urgent **(16)** .... of the growing threat **(17)** .... its unique marine life posed by global warming. Climatologists estimate that the Arctic summer has increased by five days every decade for the **(18)** .... forty years, and that a totally ice-free Arctic summer will soon occur.

The Arctic Ocean is unusual as much of it is capped **(19)** .... ice and there is land all around it. 'It is as **(20)** .... the Arctic Ocean is inside a box which has a lid of ice on the top. There's **(21)** .... other place in the world like it,' says chief scientist Ron O'Dor. A particular focus planned for the project he is undertaking **(22)** .... be the Canada Basin, an underwater hole 3,800 metres deep **(23)** .... life has remained isolated **(24)** .... millennia.

This Arctic exploration project is part of the *Census of Marine Life*, a collaboration of more than 300 scientists from 53 countries, **(25)** .... aim is to address our ignorance of what lives in the sea. **(26)** .... the Census began several years ago, more than 500 new species of fish have been identified. However, scientists believe **(27)** .... could be ten times as many yet to be discovered.

Part 3

For questions **28–37**, read the text below. Use the word given in capitals at the end of some of the lines to form a word that fits in the gap **in the same line**. There is an example at the beginning (**0**).

Write your answers **IN CAPITAL LETTERS on the separate answer sheet**.

Example:

0	T	A	L	E	N	T	E	D								

Benjamin Grosvenor

Although he's only 14, Benjamin Grosvenor is already a very **(0)** .... musician. He started playing the piano at six and soon developed an **(28)** .... ability to memorise and perform new musical pieces. At 11, he took part in the UK's *Young Musician of the Year* competition. Although he didn't win, he received many **(29)** .... reviews and was voted the audience's favourite on the competition's website. He also secured a recording deal with the record company EMI.

TALENT

IMPRESS

ENTHUSIASM

Grosvenor is clearly very pleased with the **(30)** .... he has gained, but he remains a **(31)** .... Although he captured the world's attention as an 11-year-old pianist with **(32)** .... potential, he knows that things change quickly in the **(33)** .... world of music.

RECOGNISE

REAL

STAND

COMPETE

Grosvenor has now left school and is studying at home. He is performing regularly at venues around the UK and these **(34)** .... , along with his contract with EMI, should **(35)** .... that he remains in the public eye. He practises on the piano for between six and seven hours a day and continues to display an amazing musical **(36)** .... , together with a virtually **(37)** .... technique. He has yet to release an album with EMI, but his many fans are eagerly awaiting it.

APPEAR

SURE

MATURE

FLAW

Part 4

For questions **38–42**, think of **one** word only which can be used appropriately in all three sentences. Here is an example (**0**).

Example:

0 They say the new minister is a lovely person and very .... to talk to.

My neighbours have not had a very .... life, but they always seem cheerful.

It's .... enough to see why the town is popular with tourists.

Example:

	0		E	A	S	Y												

Write **only** the missing word **IN CAPITAL LETTERS on the separate answer sheet**.

---

38 Sometimes it is better not to tell the truth if someone is likely to be ....
unnecessarily.

Considering how many vehicles were involved, it seems miraculous that no one was
.... in the accident.

It won't .... if you don't have time to iron the sheets after they've been washed.

39 The judge had a very .... sense of humour, which often surprised people as he
looked so serious.

Don't walk on the path until the concrete is ....

If you wash your hair too frequently, it may become very .... and lose all its
shine.

40 The President's 70th birthday was .... by a parade followed by a gala dinner in
the evening.

I've .... the places we should visit on the map.

At the weekend, the teacher .... over 50 student essays and prepared his
lessons for the following week.

41 These tiny reptiles can shoot poison into your .... from up to three metres away.

Never before has the ascent of this formidable mountain been attempted from the north .... in winter.

The history lecturer didn't want to lose .... by admitting he didn't know the answer.

42 I'm not sure if I can park the car in that small space but I'll have a .... at it.

A great roar went up from the crowd as the champion played a magnificent .... and won the tennis match.

All news photographers dream of taking the perfect .... that will make them famous.

Part 5

For questions **43–50**, complete the second sentence so that it has a similar meaning to the first sentence, using the word given. **Do not change the word given.** You must use between **three** and **six** words, including the word given. Here is an example (**0**).

Example:

0 James would only speak to the head of department alone.

ON

James .... to the head of department alone.

The gap can be filled with the words 'insisted on speaking', so you write:

Example: | **0** | INSISTED ON SPEAKING |

Write **only** the missing words **IN CAPITAL LETTERS on the separate answer sheet**.

---

43 David said that the accident was his fault.

TOOK

David .... the accident.

44 We would try really hard, but my older sister and I never got on.

HOW

No .... , my older sister and I never got on.

45 It might get cold when you're out this evening, so it's probably a good idea to take gloves.

CASE

It's probably worth .... cold when you're out this evening.

46 They told Nick not to go to the city centre on New Year's Eve.

WARNED

Nick .... from the city centre on New Year's Eve.

47   I wish I could have finished my biology project on time.

ABLE

I regret not .... my biology project finished on time.

48   John didn't know he had to phone his teacher if he was going to miss a class.

MEANT

John didn't know .... his teacher a call if he was going to miss a class.

49   The costs of digital photography have come down over the last few years.

DROP

There .... the costs of digital photography over the last few years.

50   I was bitterly disappointed they didn't give me a part in the school play.

BITTER

To .... given a part in the school play.

PAPER 4   LISTENING (approximately 40 minutes)

Part 1

You will hear three different extracts. For questions **1–6**, choose the answer (**A**, **B** or **C**) which fits best according to what you hear. There are two questions for each extract.

Extract One

You overhear a sportsman called Alex talking to his coach.

1   What does the coach say about motivation?

    A   Sports people have different forms of motivation.

    B   All successful sports people understand what motivates them.

    C   It is important for coaches to study the psychology of motivation.

2   Alex says he is resolved to

    A   recover his winning form.

    B   find out why he gives up so easily.

    C   focus on performing to the best of his ability.

Extract Two

You hear part of a radio programme in which a reporter called Toby Beesley is talking about a museum located in a castle.

3   Toby thinks that the people running the museum have not installed modern technology because

    A   they are unwilling to do so.

    B   they lack the means to do so.

    C   they've not been allowed to do so.

4   He recommends this museum to people who appreciate

    A   an uncomplicated display.

    B   a traditional approach.

    C   comfortable facilities.

Extract Three

You hear part of an interview with Adam Harrabin, who uses a metal detector, a hand-held machine which can discover metal buried in the ground.

5   When he answers the presenter's first question, Adam is

    A describing how the machine works.

    B estimating the value of objects he's found.

    C justifying action taken during his investigation.

6   What does Adam most enjoy about using his metal detector?

    A the thrill of finding something very old

    B the variety of places to be explored

    C the need to keep a location secret

Part 2

You will hear part of a programme in which an Australian sheep farmer called Keith Reid is talking about a local event known as the Morongla Sheepdog Trials. For questions **7–14**, complete the sentences.

THE MORONGLA SHEEPDOG TRIALS

The new Sheepdog Trials aim to raise funds to improve the

| | **7** | used for the annual country show.

Keith is very happy that a total of

| | **8** | dogs participated in the event.

In the Sheepdog Trials, teams lose points for the offence known as

| | **9** |

When the | | **10** | is closed, with the sheep inside the enclosure,

the trial is over.

Handlers may ask to begin the course again if a sheep is | | **11** |

The highest level in the Trials is called | | **12** | level.

The winning dogs will each be given a | | **13** | and some dog food.

Keith describes sheep as both | | **14** | and stubborn.

Part 3

You will hear part of an interview with an actor called Peter Jameson, who is talking about his career. For questions **15–20**, choose the answer (**A, B, C** or **D**) which fits best according to what you hear.

15   What type of roles did Peter want to play when he was younger?

    A   He was keen to specialise in famous Shakespearean parts.
    B   He thought working in television would be more rewarding.
    C   He wanted the freedom to explore a wide range of characters.
    D   He felt that classical plays would suit his personality best.

16   What do we learn about Peter's voice?

    A   He needs a microphone in order to be heard in a large venue.
    B   He makes use of the latest technology to enhance it.
    C   He finds it difficult to relax his voice when he's acting.
    D   He's learnt to get over problems through voice training.

17   According to Peter, when he took on the role of Prospero he was

    A   relieved to be playing a challenging character for a change.
    B   apprehensive at having to portray so much anger on stage.
    C   amused by the audience's reaction to his performance.
    D   doubtful as to whether he would enjoy the experience.

18   What does Peter say about learning the words in a play?

    A   He relies on the natural abilities he was born with.
    B   He's grateful for the training he received as a student.
    C   He finds it easier to remember them scene-by-scene.
    D   He accepts that memorising long parts is impossible now.

19   How does Peter feel about watching his past performances on television?

    A   He appreciates the support of friends when doing it.
    B   It's something he would rather avoid doing.
    C   There's little time for it when he's working.
    D   Being forced to do it makes him angry.

20   What particularly impressed Peter about *The Romans*?

    A   its relevance to modern times
    B   the accuracy of the historical details
    C   its original use of language
    D   the strength of the acting

Part 4

You will hear five short extracts in which students on art courses are talking about their experiences.

TASK ONE

For questions **21–25**, choose from the list (**A–H**) the difficulties each speaker has had to overcome.

TASK TWO

For questions **26–30**, choose from the list (**A–H**) what each speaker enjoys most about the process of creating art.

While you listen you must complete both tasks.

	TASK ONE		TASK TWO	
A the demands of a family	Speaker 1	**21**	**A** visualising the finished piece	Speaker 1	**26**
B a lack of work space	Speaker 2	**22**	**B** doing background reading	Speaker 2	**27**
C financial pressures	Speaker 3	**23**	**C** looking at something in detail	Speaker 3	**28**
D feelings of isolation	Speaker 4	**24**	**D** recording ideas in words	Speaker 4	**29**
E peer group pressure	Speaker 5	**25**	**E** taking photographs	Speaker 5	**30**
F poor job prospects			**F** copying the work of other artists		
G an urban environment			**G** combining different styles		
H a lack of time			**H** experimenting with colour		

PAPER 5   SPEAKING (15 minutes)

There are two examiners. One (the interlocutor) conducts the test, providing you with the necessary materials and explaining what you have to do. The other examiner (the assessor) is introduced to you, but then takes no further part in the interaction.

Part 1 (3 minutes)

The interlocutor first asks you and your partner a few questions. The interlocutor asks candidates for some information about themselves, then widens the scope of the questions by asking about e.g. candidates' leisure activities, studies, travel and daily life. Candidates are expected to respond to the interlocutor's questions and listen to what their partner has to say.

Part 2 (a one-minute 'long turn' for each candidate, plus a 30-second response from the second candidate)

You are each given the opportunity to talk for about a minute, and to comment briefly after your partner has spoken.

The interlocutor gives you a set of pictures and asks you to talk about them for about one minute. It is important to listen carefully to the interlocutor's instructions. The interlocutor then asks your partner a question about your pictures and your partner responds briefly.

You are then given another set of pictures to look at. Your partner talks about these pictures for about one minute. This time the interlocutor asks you a question about your partner's pictures and you respond briefly.

Part 3 (approximately 4 minutes)

In this part of the test you and your partner are asked to talk together. The interlocutor places a new set of pictures on the table between you. This stimulus provides the basis for a discussion. The interlocutor explains what you have to do.

Part 4 (approximately 4 minutes)

The interlocutor asks some further questions, which leads to a more general discussion of what you have talked about in Part 3. You may comment on your partner's answers if you wish.

Paper 5 Frames

Test 1

Note: In the examination, there will be both an assessor and an interlocutor in the exam. The visual material for **Test 1** appears on pages C1 and C2 (Part 2), and C3 (Part 3).

Part 1   3 minutes (5 minutes for groups of three)

Interlocutor:	Good morning/afternoon/evening. My name is .... and this is my colleague ....

And your names are?

Can I have your mark sheets, please?

Thank you.

First of all, we'd like to know something about you.

Select one or two questions and ask candidates in turn, as appropriate.

- Where are you from?
- What do you do here/there?
- How long have you been studying English?
- What do you enjoy most about learning English?

Select one or more questions from any of the following categories, as appropriate.

Money and possessions

- Are your favourite possessions the ones that cost a lot of money? ...... (Why? / Why not?)
- What is the <u>one</u> thing you own that you couldn't live without? ...... (Why?)

Music

- How important is it to share the same musical tastes as your friends? ...... (Why? / Why not?)
- How important is music in your life? ...... (Why? / Why not?)

Part 2   4 minutes (6 minutes for groups of three)

Photographers

Emotions

Interlocutor:	In this part of the test, I'm going to give each of you three pictures. I'd like you to talk about them on your own for about a minute, and also to answer a question briefly about your partner's pictures.
	(Candidate A), it's your turn first. Here are your pictures. They show **photographers working in different situations.**
	Indicate the pictures on page C1 to the candidates.
	I'd like you to compare two of the pictures, and say **what difficulties the photographers might be having, and who might be interested in the photographs they are taking.**
	All right?
Candidate A:	[*1 minute*]
Interlocutor	Thank you.
	(Candidate B), **which of the photographs being taken would be the most interesting? ...... (Why?)**
Candidate B:	[*Approximately 30 seconds*]
Interlocutor:	Thank you.
	Now, *(Candidate B)*, here are your pictures. They show **people expressing different emotions.**
	Indicate the pictures on page C2 to the candidate.
	I'd like you to compare two of the pictures, and say **how the people might be feeling, and what might have caused them to feel like this.**
	All right?
Candidate B:	[*1 minute*]
Interlocutor:	Thank you.
	(Candidate A), **which picture shows the strongest emotion? ......** **(Why?)**
Candidate A:	[*Approximately 30 seconds*]
Interlocutor:	Thank you.

Parts 3 and 4   8 minutes (12 minutes for groups of three)

Book illustrations

Part 3

Interlocutor:	Now, I'd like you to talk about something together for about three minutes. *(5 minutes for groups of three)*
	Here are some pictures illustrating the chapters of a book called 'Hopes and Fears for the Future'.
	Indicate the pictures on page C3 to the candidates.
	First, talk to each other about **what hopes and fears for the future each chapter might include.** Then decide **which chapter might interest readers most.**
	All right?
Candidates:	[*3 minutes (5 minutes for groups of three)*]
Interlocutor:	Thank you.

Part 4

Interlocutor: *Select any of the following questions, as appropriate:*

- Do you think people would buy a book like this? ...... (Why? / Why not?)
- Are television programmes more effective than books in dealing with topics like our hopes and fears for the future? ...... (Why? / Why not?)
- How important do you think illustrations in books are? ...... (Why?)
- Is it important for parents to read to their children? ...... (Why? / Why not?)
- Do you think reading books on the internet will ever replace reading printed books? ...... (Why? / Why not?)

> *Select any of the following prompts as appropriate:*
> - What do you think?
> - Do you agree?
> - How about you?

Thank you. That is the end of the test.

Test 2

Note: In the examination, there will be both an assessor and an interlocutor in the room. The visual material for **Test 2** appears on pages C4 and C5 (Part 2), and C6 (Part 3).

Part 1   3 minutes (5 minutes for groups of three)

Interlocutor: Good morning/afternoon/evening. My name is .... and this is my colleague ....

And your names are?

Can I have your mark sheets, please?

Thank you.

First of all, we'd like to know something about you.

Select one or two questions and ask candidates in turn, as appropriate.

- Where are you from?
- What do you do here/there?
- How long have you been studying English?
- What do you enjoy most about learning English?

Select one or more questions from any of the following categories, as appropriate.

Leisure time

- Are you a person who is keen on sports? ...... (Why? / Why not?)
- If you could take up a new sport or hobby, what would it be? ...... (Why? / Why not?)

Hopes for the future

- What's your greatest ambition? ...... (Why?)
- If you had the opportunity to travel anywhere in the world, where would you go? ...... (Why?)

Part 2   4 minutes (6 minutes for groups of three)

Ways of communicating

People studying

Interlocutor:	In this part of the test, I'm going to give each of you three pictures. I'd like you to talk about them on your own for about a minute, and also to answer a question briefly about your partner's pictures.
	(Candidate A), it's your turn first. Here are your pictures. They show **people communicating in different ways.**
	Indicate the pictures on page C4 to the candidates.
	I'd like you to compare two of the pictures, and say **why the people might have chosen to communicate in these ways, and how difficult it might be for them to communicate effectively.**
	All right?
Candidate A:	[*1 minute*]
Interlocutor:	Thank you.
	(Candidate B), **in which situation would it be most difficult to communicate effectively? ...... (Why?)**
Candidate B:	[*Approximately 30 seconds*]
Interlocutor:	Thank you.
	Now, *(Candidate B)*, here are your pictures. They show **people working in untidy places.**
	Indicate the pictures on page C5 to the candidates.
	I'd like you to compare two of the pictures, and say **why the people might be working in conditions like these, and what problems they might have.**
	All right?
Candidate B:	[*1 minute*]
Interlocutor:	Thank you.
	(Candidate A), **who looks the most disorganised? ...... (Why?)**
Candidate A:	[*Approximately 30 seconds*]
Interlocutor:	Thank you.

Parts 3 and 4   8 minutes (12 minutes for groups of three)

Childhood experiences

Part 3

Interlocutor:	Now, I'd like you to talk about something together for about three minutes. *(5 minutes for groups of three)*
	Here are some pictures showing different childhood experiences.
	Indicate the pictures on page C6 to the candidates.
	First, talk to each other about **why children might remember experiences like these.** Then decide **which two experiences would have the greatest influence on children's lives.**
	All right?
Candidates:	[*3 minutes (5 minutes for groups of three)*]
Interlocutor:	Thank you.

Part 4

Interlocutor: *Select any of the following questions, as appropriate:*

- People can often remember the day they first started school. Why do you think this is?
- How do young people benefit from taking part in competitive sports?
- Do you think it's true that the only way we can learn is by experience? ...... (Why? / Why not?)
- What are the advantages and disadvantages of using a computer to help you learn new things?
- Some people say that we should make an effort to experience new things throughout our lives. How far do you agree?

> *Select any of the following prompts as appropriate:*
>
> - What do you think?
> - Do you agree?
> - How about you?

Thank you. That is the end of the test.

Test 3

Note: In the examination, there will be both an assessor and an interlocutor in the room. The visual material for **Test 3** appears on pages C7 and C8 (Part 2), and C9 (Part 3).

Part 1   3 minutes (5 minutes for groups of three)

Interlocutor: Good morning/afternoon/evening. My name is .... and this is my colleague ....

And your names are?

Can I have your mark sheets, please?

Thank you.

First of all, we'd like to know something about you.

Select one or two questions and ask candidates in turn, as appropriate.

- Where are you from?
- What do you do here/there?
- How long have you been studying English?
- What do you enjoy most about learning English?

Select one or more questions from any of the following categories, as appropriate.

Money and possessions

- What would you do if you suddenly became very rich? ......
  (Why?)
- Did you save up your pocket money as a child or spend it as soon as you got it? ...... (Why?)

Hopes for the future

- How do you think learning English might help you in the future?
- What do you think you'll be doing in five years' time?

Part 2   4 minutes (6 minutes for groups of three)

People and the sea

Musical experiences

Interlocutor:	In this part of the test, I'm going to give each of you three pictures. I'd like you to talk about them on your own for about a minute, and also to answer a question briefly about your partner's pictures.

(Candidate A), it's your turn first. Here are your pictures. They show **people and the sea.**

Indicate the pictures on page C7 to the candidates.

I'd like you to compare two of the pictures, and say **why the people might have chosen to be in these situations, and how the people might be feeling.**

All right?

Candidate A: [*1 minute*]

Interlocutor: Thank you.

(Candidate B), **who seems to be enjoying the sea most? ...... (Why?)**

Candidate B: [*Approximately 30 seconds*]

Interlocutor: Thank you.

Now, *(Candidate B)*, here are your pictures. They show **people playing different types of music.**

Indicate the pictures on page C8 to the candidates.

I'd like you to compare two of the pictures, and say **what the atmosphere in these places might be like, and how the audiences might react to the music.**

All right?

Candidate B: [*1 minute*]

Interlocutor: Thank you.

(Candidate A), **which of these musical performances do you think would involve the audience the most? ...... (Why?)**

Candidate A: [*Approximately 30 seconds*]

Interlocutor: Thank you.

Parts 3 and 4   8 minutes (12 minutes for groups of three)

Taking up a career

Part 3

Interlocutor:	Now, I'd like you to talk about something together for about three minutes. *(5 minutes for groups of three)*
	Here are some pictures showing careers which young people sometimes consider taking up.
	Indicate the pictures on page C9 to the candidates.
	First, talk to each other about **what the advantages and disadvantages of taking up these careers might be.** Then decide **which one would provide the best long-term career prospects.**
	All right?
Candidates:	[*3 minutes (5 minutes for groups of three)*]
Interlocutor:	Thank you.

Part 4

Interlocutor: *Select any of the following questions, as appropriate:*

- Who do you think should be responsible for giving young people careers advice? ...... (Why?)
- What general skills are most useful for young people in the workplace? ...... (Why?)
- Which jobs do children often say they want to do? ...... (Why?)
- If you could, how would you change the education system in your country?
- What kinds of job do you think might become popular in the future? ...... (Why?)

> *Select any of the following prompts as appropriate:*
>
> - What do you think?
> - Do you agree?
> - How about you?

Thank you. That is the end of the test.

Test 4

Note: In the examination, there will be both an assessor and an interlocutor in the room. The visual material for **Test 4** appears on pages C10 and C11 (Part 2), and C12 (Part 3).

Part 1   3 minutes (5 minutes for groups of three)

Interlocutor: Good morning/afternoon/evening. My name is .... and this is my colleague ....

And your names are?

Can I have your mark sheets, please?

Thank you.

First of all, we'd like to know something about you.

Select one or two questions and ask candidates in turn, as appropriate.

- Where are you from?
- What do you do here/there?
- How long have you been studying English?
- What do you enjoy most about learning English?

Select one or more questions from any of the following categories, as appropriate.

Leisure time

- Do you think you have enough leisure time these days? ......
  (Why? / Why not?)
- Do you prefer to spend your leisure time at home or going out
  with friends? ...... (Why?)

Music

- How easy is it to go to live concerts where you live? ...... (Why? /
  Why not?)
- If you had the chance, what kind of musical instrument would
  you like to be able to play? ...... (Why?)

Part 2   4 minutes (6 minutes for groups of three)

People pointing

The five senses

Interlocutor:	In this part of the test, I'm going to give each of you three pictures. I'd like you to talk about them on your own for about a minute, and also to answer a question briefly about your partner's pictures.
	(Candidate A), it's your turn first. Here are your pictures. They show **people pointing at different things.**
	Indicate the pictures on page C10 to the candidates.
	I'd like you to compare two of the pictures, and say **why the people might have chosen to be in these situations, and how the people might be feeling.**
	All right?
Candidate A:	[*1 minute*]
Interlocutor:	Thank you.
	(Candidate B), **in which situation would the listeners need to pay the most attention? ...... (Why?)**
Candidate B:	[*Approximately 30 seconds*]
Interlocutor:	Thank you.
	Now, *(Candidate B)*, here are your pictures. They show **people using one of their five senses for different purposes.**
	Indicate the pictures on page C11 to the candidates.
	I'd like you to compare two of the pictures, and say **how the people are using their senses, and what might happen as a result.**
	All right?
Candidate B:	[*1 minute*]
Interlocutor:	Thank you.
	(Candidate A), **in which situation would the use of the senses be the most important? ...... (Why?)**
Candidate A:	[*Approximately 30 seconds*]
Interlocutor:	Thank you.

Parts 3 and 4   8 minutes (12 minutes for groups of three)

Advertising

Part 3

Interlocutor:	Now, I'd like you to talk about something together for about three minutes. *(5 minutes for groups of three)*
	Here are some advertisements which have won prizes in a competition called 'Advertisement of the Year'.
	Indicate the pictures on page C12 to the candidates.
	First, talk to each other about **what message these advertisements are trying to communicate.** Then decide **which advertisement would be the most successful in persuading people to buy the product.**
	All right?
Candidates:	[*3 minutes (5 minutes for groups of three)*]
Interlocutor:	Thank you.

Part 4

Interlocutor: *Select any of the following questions, as appropriate:*

- What do you think is more important in an advertisement – the pictures or the words? ...... (Why?)
- Do you think life would be better or worse without advertisements? ...... (Why?)
- Some people say that advertisements don't always tell the truth. What's your view?
- Apart from advertisements, in what other ways can people get information about products and services?
- What are the advantages and disadvantages of buying things on the internet?

> *Select any of the following prompts as appropriate:*
> - What do you think?
> - Do you agree?
> - How about you?

Thank you. That is the end of the test.

Marks and results

Paper 1   Reading

Candidates record their answers in pencil on a separate answer sheet. Two marks are given for each correct answer in **Parts 1, 2** and **3** and one mark is given for each correct answer in **Part 4.** The total score is then weighted to 40 marks for the whole Reading paper.

Paper 2   Writing

A General Impression Mark Scheme is used in conjunction with a Task Specific Mark Scheme, which focuses on criteria specific to each particular task. The General Impression Mark Scheme summarises the content, organisation and cohesion, range of structures and vocabulary, register and tone, and target reader indicated in each task.

A summary of the General Impression Mark Scheme is given below. Trained examiners, who are coordinated prior to each examination session, work with a more detailed version, which is subject to updating. The CAE General Impression Mark Scheme is interpreted at Council of Europe Level C1.

GENERAL IMPRESSION MARK SCHEME

5	For a **Band 5** to be awarded, the candidate's writing has a very positive effect on the target reader. The content is relevant* and the topic is fully developed. Information and ideas are skilfully organised through a range of cohesive devices, which are used to good effect. A wide range of complex structures and vocabulary is used effectively. Errors are minimal, and inaccuracies which do occur have no impact on communication. Register and format are consistently appropriate to the purpose of the task and the audience.
4	For a **Band 4** to be awarded, the candidate's writing has a positive effect on the target reader. The content is relevant* and the topic developed. Information and ideas are clearly organised through the use of a variety of cohesive devices. A good range of complex structures and vocabulary is used. Some errors may occur with vocabulary and when complex language is attempted, but these do not cause difficulty for the reader. Register and format are usually appropriate to the purpose of the task and the audience.
3	For a **Band 3** to be awarded, the candidate's writing has a satisfactory effect on the target reader. The content is relevant* with some development of the topic. Information and ideas are generally organised logically, though cohesive devices may not always be used appropriately. A satisfactory range of structures and vocabulary is used, though word choice may lack precision. Errors which do occur do not cause difficulty to the reader. Register and format are reasonably appropriate to the purpose of the task and the audience.
2	For a **Band 2** to be awarded, the candidate's writing has a negative effect on the target reader. The content is not always relevant. Information and ideas are inadequately organised and sometimes incoherent, with inaccurate use of cohesive devices. The range of structures and vocabulary is limited and/or repetitive, and errors may be basic or cause difficulty for the reader. Register and format are sometimes inappropriate to the purpose of the task and the audience.
1	For a **Band 1** to be awarded, the candidate's writing has a very negative effect on the target reader. The content is often irrelevant. Information and ideas are poorly organised, often incoherent, and there is minimal use of cohesive devices. The range of structures and vocabulary is severely limited, and errors frequently cause considerable difficulty for the reader. Register and format are inappropriate to the purpose of the task and the audience.
0	For a **Band zero** to be awarded, there is either too little language for assessment or the candidate's writing is totally irrelevant or illegible.

*   Candidates who do not address all the content points will be penalised for dealing inadequately with the requirements of the task. Candidates who fully satisfy the **Band 3** descriptor will demonstrate an adequate performance in writing at CAE level.

Paper 2 sample answers and examiner's comments

Sample A (Test 1, Question 1 – Letter)

Hi Alex.

I've just recieved your e-mail and looked through the two adverts. As you said, both of them looks good and they appear to me.

If we applied for a job in Joe's Italian restaurant, considering that we can speak a certain level of English, we would be working as waiters. It says the restaurant is located in Central London and has international staff, so I think it would be great experience as well as brushing up our English. Although pay's not great and also we have to pay for our accomodation, the budget for traveling could be tight. Well, thinking about money, Tall tree Campsite looks much more attractive.

I can imagine what it's look like and I suppose we will work as cleaners or camp organiser assistants, but it would be quite remote area from other cities and I'm afraid that there is not many things to see.

If you ask me, I fancy this Italian restaurant. Actually both would be good for English but living and working in a remote holiday resort wouldn't be nice for sightseeing and we could easily fed up with that kind of small town. Although we have to take a firm grip for living cost, I think it is better to choose staying in London and watching the big city inside. Assuming most of big museums and galleries in London are free, sighsteeing wouldn't cost very much.

Well, this is just my opinion, and I want to know what you think

Think carefully and send me a e-mail in few days.

See you.

with love,

Comments

Content
Content is relevant and developed.

Organisation and cohesion
Whilst generally logically organised, cohesive devices are not always used successfully, e.g. *although*.

Range and accuracy
Some ambitious choices of vocabulary occasionally lacking in precision. A number of errors which are non-impeding.

Register/Tone
Reasonably appropriate.

Target reader
Satisfactory effect.

Band 3

Sample B (Test 1, Question 3 – Essay)

In most homes today you will find only one generation living together. However, in some families different generations choose to live together in the same house. What is the reason for this choice, and which advantages or disadvantages might such a solution give?

The positive aspect could be that the members of the family get to know each other very well. The children in the family can be close not only to their parents, but also to their grandparents. In this way they can get the opportunity to learn about both the past and the present.

Another advantage is that the parents might have easy access to babysitters. Most grandparents like to be together with their grandchildren on their own. It is something that gives their life and added value. Many children also love to spend time with their grandparents. As grandparents they are not directly responsible for the upbringing, and can thus be more relaxed.

On the other hand, the disadvantages might be that the family members get too close, and that each member loose their privacy. It is often more difficult to say no to someone you are close to, than to others. Family members may feel they have the right to visit whenever they like and that they have the right to critizise or say their opinion without being asked.

All in all, there are both positive and negative aspects related to living together – one has to decide what is best for oneself.

Comments

Content
Content is relevant and fully developed.

Organisation and cohesion
Clearly organised; a variety of cohesive devices used appropriately.

Range and accuracy
A good range of vocabulary with minimal devices used appropriately. A good range of complex structures with occasional inaccuracies.

Register/Tone
Consistently appropriate to purpose and audience.

Target reader
Very positive effect.

Band 5

Sample C (Test 2, Question 1 – Letter)

Dear Mrs Alison Riley,

I am writing this letter in order to make some comments on behalf of the collegues, who have recently visited your studio.

First of all, the part we all disliked most concerned the discussion on studio history. It took a lot of time, the subject didn't catch the student's interest and as a result it was very boring. In addition to this, the time we had to find out about lighting and sound was very limited. A lot of the collegues had come to the studio because they were interested in learning about this specific section.

The best point of our visit that appealed to me, was the one in which the special effects were mentioned. It was my favourite, as I understood their great importance in a film. Everybody liked most the meeting with famous actors, as they were all asking for autographs.

My suggestions in order to be improved is to reduce the time which is spent on the discussion and extend the time about lighting and sound.

I hope my proposals will help you to be improved.

Yours sincerely,

Comments

Content
Content is relevant and developed.

Organisation and cohesion
Information and ideas are clearly organised. A variety of cohesive devices is used appropriately.

Range and accuracy
A good range of vocabulary and a wide range of structures are used effectively. Some non-impeding errors occur when more complex language is attempted.

Register/Tone
Register/tone are consistently appropriate.

Target reader
Positive effect on target reader.

Band 4

Sample D (Test 2, Question 5 – Report)

To: The College Library
From: XXX
Subject: "The Pelican Brief" as a thriller
Date: 7th December 2008

<u>Introduction</u>

The aim of this report is to comment on the thriller 'The Pelican Brief" and to present the ingredients of a good thriller.

<u>Thrillers</u>

It appears to all that a good thriller depends on its plot. This part should be interesting and not reveal much elements from the beginning. Furthermore, the scenery and the actors should be suitable. The action is generally appealing when it is fast and

<u>The Pelican Brief</u>

As far as "The Pelican Brief" as a choice is concerned I would strongly recommend that it will be bought as it is one of the most attractive thrillers of all the ages. The fact that actors like Julia Roberts and Denzel Washington are starring is on its own a beneficial factor. Their talent is well-known. There is a lot of mystery in the film and the audience will certainly be attracted. It would also appeal many spectators due to the fact it refers to university students as well as to policemen, professors and simple people.

<u>Conclusion</u>

I feel strongly that this thriller should be in the college library as it is a classic thriller. There is no much use of blood or violence so it can be watched with safety.

Comments

Content
Content relevant with some development.

Organisation and cohesion
Information and ideas are generally logically organised with appropriate report format used.

Range and accuracy
Satisfactory range of vocabulary and structures. Word choice lacks precision in places. Errors are non-impeding.

Register/Tone
Register/tone reasonably appropriate to purpose and audience.

Target reader
Satisfactory effect on target reader.

Band 3

Sample E (Test 3, Question 1 – Report)

> *Introduction*
>
> *The aim of this report is to let you know how it was the activity centre and if it's appropriate for working there.*
>
> *Disadvantages*
>
> *The trip on Monday was very exhausting and the centre was far away that I get really tired. Moreover at night I couldn't sleep because it had a lot of noise and that is a great disadvantage. Another thing that I should mention is that it has a lot of children with whom it's very difficult to supervise.*
>
> *As for the activities, on Friday we went children for riding and we were outside all day. Luckily we didn't went for canoeing that day.*
>
> *Advantages*
>
> *On Sunday the group was great and we had a lot of fun. That was the most quiet day of all! Another advantage that it should be mentioned is that I practised my English and now I can speak more Fluently.*
>
> *Conclusion*
>
> *Concluding the advantages and the disadvantages that I mentioned above, I believe that it has some difficulties but it is a great experience. I recommend you to go, it's worth.*

Comments

Content
Content is relevant with some development.

Organisation and cohesion
Information and ideas are generally logically organised; use of cohesive devices is limited.

Range and accuracy
Range of vocabulary and structures is limited and errors are basic and frequent.

Register/Tone
Register/tone are reasonably appropriate to purpose and audience.

Target reader
Negative effect on target reader.

Band 2

Sample F (Test 3, Question 3 – Article)

Clothes reveal people's personalities

Some people believe that the clothes someone wears, can reveal a lot of things about his personality. In other words, they are a "mirror" of each people's soul and they give a lot of information about his character. But, can all these statements be taken seriously? The answer is yes.

We can understand a lot of things only by looking the way someone is dressed. For instance, if someone is always dressed with smart clothes, or with clothes which are in fashion, we can understand that this person wants always to look great or attractive. He is taking care of himself and wants always to stand out.

On the other hand, if someone is always dressed with the same clothes, or with old-fashioned clothes and he doesn't care about his appearance, it is clear that this person may not also care about his friends or family. He may also believe that the appearance is not the only thing that matters, so he has other priorities in his life.

This phenomenon is not weird. We can understand a lot of things about each person's character because his clothes and the accessories which he probably wears, make it clear to us. So, every time you get dressed, take care, because anyone will be able to understand the same things about your personality.

Comments

Content
Content is relevant and developed.

Organisation and cohesion
Information and ideas are clearly organised; cohesive devices are generally used appropriately.

Range and accuracy
A satisfactory range of vocabulary and structures is used; errors are non-impeding and do not cause difficulty for the reader.

Register/Tone
Register/tone are usually appropriate to purpose and audience.

Target reader
Positive effect on target reader.

Band 4

Sample G *(Test 4, Question 1 – Letter)*

Dear Jan,

how are you? I was really pleased when I received your letter! I found out that you are interested in taking part in the same English course as I did, so I decided to provide you some information about it.

First of all I believe that you'll love the place! The location where we stayed was great and the people were really friendly! What is more, the area was accessible and the shops had reasonable prices.

In the main course he had to do grammar classes for about 2 hours, which was a little bit boring as all of us had already studied lots of grammar. But, after that we could participate in conversation classes, which was really useful, because we had the opportunity to do some speaking practice and at the same time make new friends!

We had a visit in Oxford, too. Although it was rather expensive and not included in the course fees, it was very interesting!

Finally, I believe that the best part of the course was the trip in London. It was super! The museums were great and with free entrance. You know, some of the students didn't speak English and it was a little bit annoying, but not enough to ruin our time there!

All in all the course was interesting and helpful! We were able to practice our English and discover the UK. So, I strongly recomment it to you! There are some hidden costs, however it is a unique and lifetime experience!

Take care,

your friend

Comments

Content
Content is relevant and developed.

Organisation and cohesion
Information and ideas are generally logically organised with some over-paragraphing. A variety of cohesive devices is used appropriately.

Range and accuracy
A good range of vocabulary is used with some evidence of collocation and expression. A satisfactory range of structures is used; errors are non-impeding and do not cause difficulty for the reader.

Register/Tone
Register/tone are consistently appropriate to purpose and audience.

Target reader
Positive effect on target reader.

Band 4

Sample H (Test 4, Question 2 – Essay)

What makes a music star successful

Nowadays, there are a lot of music stars, who are singing great hits and are famous worldwide. The question tha arise is, the image and good marketing that make him famous or is it the music?

First of all, it is known that we are more easily attracted by the beautiful people, so being beautiful could really help someone be famous. In addition, the stereotypes that exists today want almost everyone who is famous throw the music world to be gorgeous.

Moreover, it is really important that their producers will do a good marketing campaign, otherwise no matter how talented someone may be it would be really difficult to get noticed. We should not forget that in most cases the media are those who make someone famous or crash him down.

On the other hand, the singer also needs to be talented. If the singer or the musician is not at all talented, he might be famous at first, but when his fans will go to see him live, they will understand that he is not worthing his good reputation. Furthermore it is likely that neither any producer will want to have him as client, because he does not see the point of trying to change someone who is completly untalented into a star.

All in all, it seems, that nowadays if someone wants to be a music star, he does not only need to have the right connections or to be beautiful and have a good promotion, but he also has to be skillful and talented.

Comments

Content
Content is relevant with some development.

Organisation and cohesion
Information and ideas are clearly organised; a variety of cohesive devices is used appropriately.

Range and accuracy
A good range of vocabulary is used but word choice lacks precision in places.
A good range of structures is attempted; errors are non-impeding and do not cause difficulty for the reader.

Register/Tone
Register/tone are usually appropriate to purpose and audience.

Target reader
Satisfactory effect on target reader.

Band 3

Paper 3   Use of English

One mark is given for each correct answer in **Parts 1, 2** and **3**. Two marks are given for each correct answer in **Part 4**. For **Part 5**, candidates are awarded a mark of 2, 1 or 0 for each question according to the accuracy of their response. Correct spelling is required in **Parts 2, 3, 4** and **5**. The total mark is subsequently weighted to 40.

Paper 4   Listening

One mark is given for each correct answer. The total is weighted to give a mark out of 40 for the paper.

For security reasons, several versions of the Listening paper are used at each administration of the examination. Before grading, the performance of the candidates in each of the versions is compared and marks adjusted to compensate for any imbalance in levels of difficulty.

Paper 5   Speaking

Candidates are assessed on their own individual performance and not in relation to each other, according to the following five analytical criteria: grammatical resource, vocabulary resource, discourse management, pronunciation and interactive communication. Assessment is based on performance in the whole test and not in particular parts of the test.

Both examiners assess the candidates. The assessor applies detailed analytical scales, and the interlocutor applies a global achievement scale, which is based on the analytical scales.

Analytical scales

Grammatical resource

This refers to the accurate and appropriate use of a range of both simple and complex forms. Performance is viewed in terms of the overall effectiveness of the language used in spoken interaction.

Vocabulary resource

This refers to the candidate's ability to use a wide range of vocabulary to meet task requirements. At CAE level, the tasks require candidates to speculate and exchange views on unfamiliar topics. Performance is viewed in terms of the overall effectiveness of the language used in spoken interaction.

Discourse management

This refers to the candidate's ability to link utterances together to form coherent speech, without undue hesitation. The utterances should be relevant to the tasks and should be arranged logically to develop the themes or arguments required by the tasks.

Pronunciation

This refers to the candidate's ability to produce intelligible utterances to fulfil the task requirements. This includes stress and intonation as well as individual sounds. Examiners put themselves in the position of the non-ESOL specialist and assess the overall impact of the pronunciation and the degree of effort required to understand the candidate.

Interactive communication

This refers to the candidate's ability to take an active part in the development of the discourse. This requires the ability to participate in the range of interactive situations in the test and to develop discussions on a range of topics by initiating and responding appropriately. This also refers to the deployment of strategies to maintain interaction at an appropriate level throughout the test so that the tasks can be fulfilled.

Global achievement

This refers to the candidate's overall effectiveness in dealing with the tasks in the four separate parts of the CAE Speaking test. The global mark is an independent, impression mark which reflects the assessment of the candidate's performance from the interlocutor's perspective.

Marks

Marks for each of the criteria are awarded out of a five-point scale. Marks for the Speaking test are subsequently weighted to produce a final mark out of 40.

CAE typical minimum adequate performance

The candidate develops the interaction with contributions which are mostly coherent and extended when dealing with the CAE-level tasks. Grammar is mostly accurate and vocabulary appropriate. Utterances are understood with very little strain on the listener.

Test 1 Key

Paper 1 Reading (1 hour 15 minutes)

Part 1

1 D   2 C   3 B   4 D   5 A   6 B

Part 2

7 G   8 E   9 A   10 C   11 F   12 D

Part 3

13 A   14 C   15 D   16 B   17 B   18 A   19 B

Part 4

20 D   21 A   22 B   23 E   24 D   25 C   26 A   27 B   28 D   29 B
30 A   31 E   32 D   33 C   34 D

Paper 2 Writing (1 hour 30 minutes)

Task-specific Mark Schemes

The accuracy of language, including spelling and punctuation, is assessed on the general impression scale for all tasks. Criteria for assessing specific range of language and task achievement are outlined below.

Part I

The focus of Part 1 is on content, effective organisation of the input, appropriacy of the piece(s) of writing to the intended audience, and on accuracy. Some use of key words from the input is acceptable, but candidates should have reworded phrases as far as possible. The range will be defined by the task.

Question 1

Content (points covered)
The candidate's **letter** must:
- compare the two jobs
- say which job they think is better for the two friends
- give reasons for their opinion(s).
Points may be embedded or implicit.

Organisation and cohesion
Clearly organised into paragraphs with appropriate linking devices.
Letter format with suitable opening and closing formulae.
Early reference to reason for writing.

Range
Language of description, justification and recommendation.
Vocabulary related to work and leisure.

Register/Tone
Informal to unmarked. Must be consistent.

Friendly informative tone.

Target reader
Would be informed.

Part 2

In Part 2, candidates have more scope to display their linguistic competence and there is more latitude in the interpretation of the task. The assessment focus is mainly on content, range, and style/register, with attention paid to how successfully the candidate has produced the text type required.

Question 2

Content
The candidate's **report** should describe typical school, outline strengths of typical school(s) and suggest improvements. (Accept reference to any educational establishment.)

Organisation and cohesion
Clearly organised into paragraphs with appropriate linking devices. Headings may be an advantage.

Range
Language of description and suggestion/recommendation.
Vocabulary related to education.

Register/Tone
Formal to unmarked. Must be consistent.

Target reader
Would be informed.

Question 3

Content
The candidate's **essay** should explain the advantages and disadvantages of different generations living together.

Organisation and cohesion
Clearly organised into paragraphs with appropriate linking devices.

Range
Language of explanation, opinion and justification.
Vocabulary related to lifestyles/social and national customs.

Register/Tone
Formal to unmarked. Must be consistent.

Target reader
Would be informed.

Question 4

Content
The candidate's **article** should discuss whether people give presents because they want to or because of commercial or social pressures, and describe what makes a good present.

Organisation and cohesion
Clearly organised into paragraphs with appropriate linking devices.

Range
Language of evaluation, description and opinion.
Vocabulary related to present-giving/celebrations.

Register/Tone
May mix registers if appropriate to approach taken by candidate.

Target reader
Would be informed.

Question 5 (a)

Content
The candidate's **review** should explain whether the plot of *The Pelican Brief* is realistic, give reasons and say if they would recommend the thriller to other readers.

Organisation and cohesion
Clearly organised into paragraphs with appropriate linking devices.

Range
Language of description, explanation/justification and recommendation.
Vocabulary related to 'thriller' genre.

Register/Tone
May mix registers if appropriate to approach taken by candidate.

Target reader
Would be informed.

Question 5 (b)

Content
The candidate's **review** should describe an event from *Lucky Jim* which is funny, say how this event affects the rest of the story and say whether other people would enjoy *Lucky Jim*.

Organisation and cohesion
Clearly organised into paragraphs with appropriate linking devices.

Range
Language of description, explanation and opinion.
Vocabulary related to humour.

Register/Tone
May mix registers if appropriate to approach taken by candidate.

Target reader
Would be informed.

Paper 3   Use of English (1 hour)

Part 1

1 C   **2** B   **3** D   **4** A   **5** B   **6** D   **7** A   **8** B   **9** C   **10** D   **11** B   **12** C

Part 2

13 Unlike   **14** which   **15** from   **16** To   **17** due/owing/thanks
18 unless/before/until   **19** enough   **20** no/little   **21** with   **22** all   **23** that
24 any/every   **25** being   **26** far   **27** Though/Although/While/Whilst

Part 3

28 accessible   29 passionately   30 recordings   31 unexpectedly   32 surprisingly
33 exceptionally   34 enriches   35 expertise   36 memorable   37 simplicity

Part 4

38 covered   39 false   40 branch   41 touched   42 account

Part 5

43 failed to realise | the importance / significance   44 is believed | to have been   45 is
responsible for | locking   46 was his inability | to come   47 is not worth | (us/our) going
swimming / going to swim   48 gave (me) | such helpful advice OR 's advice was such a help
49 had not put off | buying   50 likely to return | having (now) seen OR likely to return |
(after) having seen

Paper 4   Listening (approximately 40 minutes)

Part 1

1 C   2 A   3 C   4 B   5 B   6 A

Part 2

7 heart monitor   8 (golf) umbrella   9 sandstorm   10 noodles   11 (mobile) phone / mobile
12 dragons / a dragon   13 postcards   14 website

Part 3

15 C   16 D   17 D   18 A   19 B   20 D

Part 4

21 G   22 B   23 F   24 C   25 A   26 H   27 E   28 D   29 B   30 F

Transcript   *This is the Cambridge Certificate in Advanced English Listening Test. Test One. I'm
going to give you the instructions for this test. I'll introduce each part of the test and
give you time to look at the questions.*

At the start of each piece you'll hear this sound:

tone

You'll hear each piece twice.

*Remember, while you're listening, write your answers on the **question paper**. You'll
have **five minutes** at the end of the test **to copy your answers onto the separate
answer sheet**.*

*There'll now be a pause. Please ask any questions now, because you must not speak
during the test.*

[pause]

PART 1   *Now open your question paper and look at Part One.*

                      [pause]

                      You'll hear three different extracts. For questions one to six, choose the answer (A, B, or C) which fits best according to what you hear. There are two questions for each extract.

Extract 1   *You hear a reporter talking to a scientific illustrator at an exhibition of his work. Now look at questions one and two.*

                      [pause]

                      tone

Reporter: Good evening, Mr Delgado. Would you mind answering one or two questions for the Daily Gazette?
Delgado: A pleasure.
Reporter: I understand you first embarked on your career as a scientific illustrator twenty-five years ago?
Delgado: Quite correct – though I once doubted work would come my way, it always has. I began with a series of paintings of moths. I felt I had a mission to help people share my love of the whole insect world, not just pretty things like butterflies, using the new computer skills I'd previously mastered.
Reporter: And you really succeeded. This is a wonderful exhibition, Mr Delgado.
Delgado: You didn't have any problem finding the venue? The streets around here are fascinating but not always easy to get to if you don't know the area.
Reporter: I have to admit I did lose my way in the car! But as soon as I entered the building, I was delighted by the beauty of your illustrations – right from your earliest. Of course, I appreciate you've had to be selective.
Delgado: Impossible otherwise.
Reporter: And I must commend the lighting – so sensitively placed for the fullest effect.

                      [pause]

                      tone

                      [The recording is repeated.]

                      [pause]

Extract 2   *You hear two journalists, Catherine and Tomas, talking about their work. Now look at questions three and four.*

                      [pause]

                      tone

Catherine: Hi, Tomas, you look very relaxed, I must say. No deadlines looming on the horizon?
Tomas: For once in my life, I'm up to date, so I can take the afternoon off and spend some quality time with the kids. I find I can churn out pieces twice as quickly, now that our new editor has realised we should have more free rein subject-wise.

Catherine: Absolutely. I used to hate being told at our regular meetings: 'You will work on subject X or whatever ... .' Oh no! Like you, I can get up at the crack of dawn to work on a story when it's something that grips me.

Tomas: Absolutely, and there's so much more to choose from now. Go back a couple of decades and your average top-quality journalist had to deliver weighty news stories, whereas now we have more space to reflect on issues and actually show that we're involved.

Catherine: But that doesn't mean that journalism is any more truthful than it was. If anything, it's the opposite. Everyone wants their angle to be promoted.

[pause]

tone

[The recording is repeated.]

[pause]

Extract 3   *You hear part of an interview with a zoologist called Roger Bonham. Now look at questions five and six.*

[pause]

tone

Interviewer: So, could you tell us about your work at the zoo?

Roger: Exotic creatures from the world may still be the attraction for many visitors; there's nothing like the birth of a new lion cub, for example, to bring the crowds in, but we're also becoming home to many British wild animals. Various feathered, furry and winged creatures have just 'sneaked in', taken up residence alongside the non-native animals, and I've been identifying, counting and recording them. What we need to do is get some finance in place to take this further.

Interviewer: And what are your concerns for the future?

Roger: In my opinion, the school network system we set up is working and children who are brought up in an urban environment get the chance to see zebra, giraffe, etc. I'm concerned, though, in Britain we haven't really got enough protected wild areas for animals to thrive in. There's increasing evidence that there are worrying fluctuations in the population of many rare native species; partly due to pollution, but chiefly due to increasing urbanisation.

Interviewer: And you want to be able to keep an eye on that?

Roger: That's right.

[pause]

tone

[The recording is repeated.]

[pause]

That's the end of Part One.
Now turn to Part Two.

[pause]

PART 2

You'll hear a woman called Jill Arthur giving a talk about walking across the Gobi Desert in Asia. For questions 7 to 14, complete the sentences. You now have 45 seconds to look at Part Two.

[pause]

tone

Jill: I'm here today to tell you about my amazing trip across the Gobi Desert in China – on foot! It was presented as a challenge in a daily newspaper, a 30-day trek, but with back-up all along the route – tents set up at night and so on.

Now it might come as a surprise to hear that I've never had a personal trainer and I don't consider myself a sportswoman, I'm actually a computer operator but I'd always wanted to see the world. So, when I read the article, I thought, 'Here's my chance,' so I applied for the trip and took three months off work.

I was totally unfit – at first that was – with some minor problems. Last November I just started walking everywhere around London with a bottle of water and what's called a heart monitor. This allowed me to check that I was building up my stamina each week.

I have to confess I'm not at all practical and I'd never been camping before. When I was shopping for my sleeping bag, I saw a huge golf umbrella and thought, 'That'll be handy to keep off the sun.' Actually it was very awkward to carry and I ditched it on the first day.

When we first arrived, we could see the sky looked dark – as if it was going to rain. In fact there was a sandstorm all that night, so I hardly slept a wink, and I got up looking messier than ever before. You couldn't see my eyes and my hair was standing on end!

Anyway, I soon got used to things – our programme was really well organised. After a day's walk, we'd suddenly see a truck on the horizon with tables, chairs, cutlery – and someone had made, not rice as you might expect, but noodles for us followed by poached pears. We just got looked after so well.

We were never out of contact with the organisers. We found that we couldn't rely on a mobile phone – we were hundreds of kilometres from any big centres of population – but we were in contact by radio in case of emergency.

The Gobi Desert is quite crunchy to walk on – not soft like the Sahara – and there's lots to see. There are salt lakes and the wind creates wonderful shapes in the sand that are always changing. Some people think that they see pyramids, others castles, but on our trip they resembled dragons.

Sometimes we came to villages. The people were very hospitable and gave us bread and tea and let us sleep in their homes. The only extra luggage I'd taken with me were a few postcards to hand out as gifts and some photographs of my family, which fascinated them.

The experience was unforgettable – the companionship, exhaustion and exhilaration of completing the journey. When I came back I wrote articles for newspapers and magazines and received a number of letters from people wanting more information. So I set up a website. I'm pleased to say it won a prize in a travel magazine!

[pause]

Now you'll hear the recording again.

tone

[The recording is repeated.]

[pause]

That's the end of Part Two.
Now turn to Part Three.

[pause]

PART 3

You'll hear part of an interview with a singer-songwriter called Nick Chalke, who is talking about his career. For questions 15 to 20, choose the answer (A, B, C or D) which fits best according to what you hear. You now have one minute to look at Part Three.

[pause]

tone

Presenter: Today I'm interviewing Nick Chalke, singer-songwriter and instrumentalist, whose prodigious new work is released this week. Called *Blue Guitars*, it's a collection of no fewer than eleven CDs. This is an enormous project, Nick, 134 new songs in only two years. How did it come about?

Nick: I think what it was, I felt like I'd been let off the leash – given a bit of space to do my own thing. When I first started, the only way I could get known was as a guy who sang quiet songs at a grand piano. It took five years of solid touring, fronting a rock band as a vocalist and guitarist, to turn that image around. The only reason I stayed with rock was because that's what brought in the crowds and kept the bank account healthy.

Presenter: It must have been a marathon getting all the recordings done.

Nick: Oh yeah. Each CD took a month to record – that was our limit. I'm not with a band any more, so the studio brought in musicians to provide the instrumentals – usual arrangement, they get a share of the royalty payments. Two or three of them were really fed up because they'd bring in their new expensive guitar that supposedly does everything and can be plugged into a computer, and we'd explain it just didn't suit the genre. They needed some convincing, that's for sure.

Presenter: Now, about ten years ago, you were offered a contract to record duets with a couple of younger pop stars, who shall be nameless. Why didn't you take it up?

Nick: It could have put me back in the spotlight, and there was a lot of money on the table, but I knew I couldn't handle the sort of haggling that's a feature of the music world – I was between agents at the time and had to do my own negotiating. My wife said, 'Don't do it' and I realised she knew exactly what she was talking about.

Presenter: So you play what people call 'the blues'. What's your definition of that term?

Nick: All through my career, I've had arguments about this with rock journalists who claim it's got to have musical connotations – they *would* say that, wouldn't they! For me, pure and simple, it's an emotion which is harrowing or tragic, and I believe that everyone in the world is capable of having the blues at some time or other. Transferring that into music is what I do.

Presenter: What's your technique for writing songs?

Nick: I start thinking about it first thing in the morning. I'm in the kitchen, which is like a madhouse, with the kids telling me jokes and things until they all head for the school bus. Then I pour myself a cup of coffee, put some music on and can just gaze out the window. I'm barely aware of the view – I'm looking inside myself. Something happens in that quiet hour without fail, and I try it out at the piano later. Of course, it may not be any good. But by nightfall it's all there.

Presenter: When you're writing, how do you know if you've come up with a really good song?

Nick: When you sing what you're thinking and it all happens at once. Then you immediately panic, thinking someone else must have thought of it first – though, of course, people do borrow the odd phrase all the time, and there are no new storylines at all! I'm unusual in that I don't think a good song is one that listeners necessarily relate to on a personal level – they don't even need to be able to whistle the tune after one hearing!

Presenter: Now on the covers of your new CD collection ...

[pause]

Now you'll hear the recording again.

tone

[The recording is repeated.]

[pause]

That's the end of Part Three.
Now turn to Part Four.

[pause]

PART 4   *Part Four consists of two tasks. You'll hear five short extracts in which people are talking about their jobs. Look at Task 1. For questions 21 to 25, choose from the list A to H the reason each speaker gives for choosing their current job. Now look at Task 2. For questions 26 to 30, choose from the list A to H the problem each speaker encounters in their current job. While you listen you must complete both tasks. You now have 45 seconds to look at Part Four.*

[pause]

tone

Speaker One   I was never too keen on simply shuttling up and down the national motorways, so when they offered me this job I took it like a shot. I've been lucky and got to visit quite a few countries. My wife doesn't mind too much – she plays in darts tournaments, so she's often away herself. So I'll probably go on doing this till I retire. I do find it frustrating queuing at border checkpoints, though. They inspect this and stamp that, and you just have to sit in your cab for hours on end, until things start moving. Makes it hard to tell how long a trip will take. But what can you do?

[pause]

Speaker Two   The book the film's based on has always been a family favourite. Mum says I'm just like Linda, the heroine. During my year off before university, when I was travelling in Mexico, I heard they were going to make a film, and I knew straightaway I had to go for the role. Mum thought I was really cheeky because I'd never done any acting before, but actually I'd always harboured a secret ambition to have a go – well, anyway, they gave me the part. But it's tricky keeping up my college work as well. I'm writing history essays on a laptop while sitting waiting for my make-up to be done, and some nights I have to stay up pretty late to catch up.

[pause]

Speaker Three   Becoming a farmer was a foregone conclusion. I was the eldest son, and it was always understood that I'd take over when the time came. We're permanently fretting about money, of course. For the past few years, we've been saying things can't get worse, but they have! There's not much more I can cut back on – everything's pared to the bone as it is. It's a hard life, takes all the hours of the day, and night too, sometimes, but if I have a bit of free time, I play a bit of chess on the computer.

[pause]

Speaker Four   Originally I was a newspaper photographer, but I have this passion for all kinds of aircraft – I used to make models and attend air shows – so that gave me a bit of specialist knowledge, and now I shoot stills and moving footage of old planes, from the air. My family tried to put me off, because they thought it'd be dangerous, but it isn't. Still, I do have to get up early, to assess my chances of getting airborne – UK weather is so changeable that it can go from good to poor in only two hours! The meteorological office do their best, I suppose. I get my daughter off to school …

[pause]

Speaker Five   You see, I've been a regular at the café since childhood, and when the owner said he was thinking of selling, I jumped at the chance. My wife Susan's been very supportive, but the place is still a building site. Sometimes I wonder if I should have stayed in the army. But I'd done twenty years and I was going nowhere, so I decided to opt out and find something with more of a future. Home for us and the kids is upstairs, above the café. The only hitch is, there's barely room to turn around. Who knows how long we'll stay? But I hope we can bring in enough money to make a go of it.

[pause]

Now you'll hear the recording again.

tone

[The recording is repeated.]

[pause]

That's the end of Part Four.

*There'll now be a pause of **five minutes** for you to **copy your answers onto the separate answer sheet**. Be sure to follow the numbering of all the questions. I'll remind you when there's one minute left, so that you're sure to finish in time.*

[Teacher, pause the recording here for five minutes. Remind your students when they have one minute left.]

That's the end of the test. Please stop now. Your supervisor will now collect all the question papers and answer sheets.

Test 2 Key

Paper 1   Reading (1 hour 15 minutes)

Part 1

1 D   2 A   3 B   4 D   5 B   6 A

Part 2

7 B   8 G   9 D   10 E   11 A   12 C

Part 3

13 C   14 C   15 B   16 D   17 B   18 A   19 B

Part 4

20 D   21 C   22 A   23 D   24 A   25 D   26 C   27 A   28 C   29 B
30 D   31 B   32 D   33 B   34 A

Paper 2   Writing (1 hour 30 minutes)

Task-specific Mark Schemes

The accuracy of language, including spelling and punctuation, is assessed on the general impression scale for all tasks. Criteria for assessing specific range of language and task achievement are outlined below.

Part I

The focus of Part 1 is on content, effective organisation of the input, appropriacy of the piece(s) of writing to the intended audience, and on accuracy. Some use of key words from the input is acceptable, but candidates should have reworded phrases as far as possible. The range will be defined by the task.

Question 1

Content (points covered)
The candidate's **letter** must:
- explain which aspects of the day they enjoyed
- explain what they were disappointed by
- suggest how future visits could be improved.

Organisation and cohesion
Clearly organised into paragraphs with appropriate linking devices.
Letter format with suitable opening and closing formulae.
Early reference to reason for writing.

Range
Language of explanation, evaluation, opinion and suggestion.
Vocabulary related to cinema and film making.

Register/Tone
Formal to unmarked. Polite persuasive tone.

Target reader
Would be informed.

Part 2

In Part 2, candidates have more scope to display their linguistic competence and there is more latitude in the interpretation of the task. The assessment focus is mainly on content, range, and style/register, with attention paid to how successfully the candidate has produced the text type required.

Question 2

Content
The candidate's **essay** should give opinion(s) on children owning mobile phones and justify opinion(s).

Organisation and cohesion
Clearly organised into paragraphs with appropriate linking devices.

Range
Language of description, opinion and justification.
Vocabulary related to the use of mobile phones.

Register/Tone
Any, as long as consistent.

Target reader
Would be informed.

Question 3

Content
The candidate's **competition entry** should identify the English-speaking country and justify their choice, speculate on how winning could affect their future and explain why they would be the most deserving winner.

Organisation and cohesion
Clearly organised into paragraphs with appropriate linking devices.

Range
Language of choice and reason, speculation and persuasion. Vocabulary related to language learning and further education or future work.

Register/Tone
Formal to unmarked. Must be consistent.

Target reader
Would be informed.

Question 4

Content
The candidate's **article** should tell us about one extreme sport that they would like to try, explain why and describe what type of person is attracted to extreme sports.
N.B. Candidates may already be doing this sport.

Organisation and cohesion
Clearly organised into paragraphs with appropriate linking devices.

Range
Language of description, explanation and suggestion. Vocabulary related to extreme sports.

Register/Tone
Any, as long as consistent.

Target reader
Would be informed.

Question 5 (a)

Content
The candidate's **report** should describe what makes a good thriller, say whether *The Pelican Brief* is a good thriller and give reasons.

Organisation and cohesion
Clearly organised into paragraphs with appropriate linking devices.
Headings may be an advantage.

Range
Language of description, opinion and justification.
Vocabulary related to "thriller" genre.

Register/Tone
Unmarked to formal. Must be consistent.

Target reader
Would be informed.

Question 5 (b)

Content
The candidate's **essay** should describe Jim's relationship with another character in the story and explain why this relationship is interesting.

Organisation and cohesion
Clearly organised into paragraphs with appropriate linking devices.

Range
Language of description and explanation.
Vocabulary related to relationships.

Register/Tone
Unmarked to formal. Must be consistent.

Target reader
Would be informed.

Paper 3   Use of English (1 hour)

Part 1

1 B   2 C   3 B   4 C   5 D   6 A   7 B   8 D   9 B   10 A   11 D
12 C

Part 2

13 not   14 for   15 even   16 must / will / should   17 which   18 it
19 would / does / did   20 whether / if   21 despite   22 few   23 so / thus
24 What   25 from   26 on   27 may / might / could

Part 3

28 darkens   **29** torrential   **30** spectacular   **31** undoubtedly / doubtless   **32** specialise
33 extensive   **34** accuracy   **35** advantageous   **36** increasingly   **37** continually
/ continuously

Part 4

38 process   **39** ruled   **40** power   **41** hard   **42** caught

Part 5

43 take care of his patients | in / during / throughout   **44** not to let | her children eat
45 work harder / more | than (I / I had) expected   **46** be sent tomorrow | as long as / so long
as   **47** no (other) / little choice / alternative / option | but   **48** (plans) do you have / have
you (got) | in mind   **49** got / sat / settled down | to (do / start)   **50** clear /obvious (that) | he
objected to

Paper 4   Listening (approximately 40 minutes)

Part 1

1 B   2 C   3 C   4 A   5 B   6 C

Part 2

7 courage   8 chest   9 feet / toes / paws   10 (a/the) collar / (the) collars
11 wheel   12 head   13 voice   14 (good) sleeping bag

Part 3

15 B   16 A   17 A   18 C   19 C   20 D

Part 4

21 F   22 E   23 H   24 B   25 G   26 E   27 H   28 A   29 C   30 B

Transcript   *This is the Cambridge Certificate in Advanced English Listening Test. Test Two. I'm
going to give you the instructions for this test. I'll introduce each part of the test and
give you time to look at the questions.*

At the start of each piece you'll hear this sound:

tone

You'll hear each piece twice.

*Remember, while you're listening, write your answers on the **question paper**. You'll
have **five minutes** at the end of the test to **copy your answers onto the separate
answer sheet.***

*There'll now be a pause. Please ask any questions now, because you must not speak
during the test.*

[pause]

PART 1

Now open your question paper and look at Part One.

[pause]

You'll hear three different extracts. For questions one to six, choose the answer (A, B, or C) which fits best according to what you hear. There are two questions for each extract.

Extract 1

You overhear two friends, Bill and Maria, discussing a marathon race they are both going to run in.

Now look at questions one and two.

[pause]

tone

Bill:	Hi, Maria. Are you ready for the race on Sunday?
Maria:	Well, Bill, it's my first marathon, so I'm not sure how to prepare. I'm planning to stay in on Saturday, give my legs a break and prepare mentally, but a colleague's going to run ten kilometres. I think that's risky.
Bill:	Yes, some people like to work their muscles on the track or in the gym the day before. Staying off your feet and focusing on the psychological side is what it should be all about. At least that's what I think. Now, have you got a running plan for the race itself?
Maria:	Sort of. Do the first half fast and then ease up when I start to tire.
Bill:	You think you'll know when it's time to do that? Races are very exciting things – the adrenalin takes over and it's hard to react sensibly. Sticking to an even pace from start to finish means you won't get an initial buzz but you won't fall apart after 20 kilometres either. Oh, and don't be tempted to miss out on the first drink station because you're worried about taking on too much fluid.

[pause]

tone

[The recording is repeated.]

[pause]

Extract 2

You hear part of a discussion in which two students are talking about their course in journalism.

Now look at questions three and four.

[pause]

tone

Woman:	I'm only now getting to grips with the terminology used on the course.
Man:	It takes time. And some of the lecturers get so carried away by their topic that they assume we know all the specialist terminology.
Woman:	We do tasks online too. I can work at my own pace and check out whatever I'm unsure about. The online component means you can do all sorts of options on this course. I'm getting so much out of that.
Man:	I've covered sports journalism, freelancing, international news; more in the first semester than I would have thought possible.

Woman:	If you click on *forum* on the menu on the left, there's an interesting debate going on about a journalist who broke the law by discussing a case while it was still going on. This is the stuff we seriously need to know about.
Man:	The penalties can be horrendous, a fine at best. If you started to stir something up and get an interesting story, you could find yourself in deep trouble. And the result is 'safe' stories that no one really wants to read about. No wonder sales of newspapers are going down.

[pause]

tone

[The recording is repeated.]

[pause]

Extract 3

You hear part of a radio programme about the types of books that people read.

Now look at questions five and six.

[pause]

tone

Woman:	At the moment I do so much background reading for my work as a translator. It's rewarding – don't get me wrong – but it's really intense trying to keep up with all the new shades of meaning words take on, because you need to be exact in my job or the results can be disastrous. When I get home, I just flop. I really used to enjoy fiction, but nothing's tempted me recently. So I don't particularly read for pleasure because I don't have the time.
Man:	I like Russian novels because the greatest writers deal with everyday human concerns so analytically – why do we do the things we do, how to live out an idea, etc. Other things I like reading – well, the Irish writer James Joyce. He's refreshing because he's so radical. In Joyce, you don't get the normal character description. Everything's a flow of random thoughts and connections.

[pause]

tone

[The recording is repeated.]

[pause]

That's the end of Part One.
Now turn to Part Two.

[pause]

PART 2

You'll hear a talk about the dogs that work in the Arctic. For questions 7 to 14, complete the sentences. You now have 45 seconds to look at Part Two.

[pause]

tone

One of the world's most thrilling sights is a team of dogs racing across an Arctic landscape, hauling a laden sled and its fur-clad driver from one frozen outpost to another. These dogs, well known for their courage as well as for their reliability, have always been essential to human existence in snow-bound environments, and many stories celebrate their exploits.

All sled dogs are adapted to harsh conditions, but the breeds vary. In the extreme conditions of the North, the dogs are big and heavy. In less severe climates, breeds are chosen for strength and speed. Physically, the dogs are powerfully built; their chest is deep and their shoulders are strong enough to pull great weights. To protect them against sub-zero temperatures, they have a double coat, and feet that are lower in temperature than their body, to prevent the snow forming ice balls between their toes. Their stomachs are such that they don't need to eat every day, and they're trained to feast when they can, their bodies then storing the energy.

Sled dogs' behavioural traits, inherited from their ancestors, are those of primitive pack animals. They live communally, and instinctively organise themselves into a hierarchical structure, with each animal having a defined status in the pack. This is reflected in the composition of the team where the dogs work in pairs. They're attached by ropes and collars to a line which pulls the sled. Their enthusiasm for pulling loaded sleds over great distances for days at a time is overwhelming. They're also deafeningly noisy, especially when they're getting ready for a day's work. Closest to the sled, supplying the power, are the wheel dogs, the main source of strength and energy – and a strange name, given that a sled has no wheels. Next in line and running ahead of them are the swing dogs. They are the brains of the team and they fine-tune the steering. The older dogs tend to take the lead at the head of the line, not at the back as you'd expect, because they are clever rather than strong. They're trusted for their ability to keep the sled out of trouble.

There is no steering on a dog sled and no reins, so the driver, who stands at the back of the sled, has to rely on his voice to communicate a variety of instructions to the dogs and can bring the sled to a halt with a brake which is worked by foot. There is no handbrake, however, and so if there is any reason to leave the dogs with the sled, the driver must fix an anchor into the ice, or the dogs will be off into the distance. Their only interest is keeping going, with or without their human cargo.

On long trips across the Arctic forest, sleds stop overnight at wooden huts which are known by the name 'sugar shacks', although no one could tell me why. Inside, the drivers sleep, the dogs curling up outside the shacks in the snow with only their thick fur coats for protection. They really are wonderfully adapted to their frozen environment. Much better than the drivers who couldn't survive the night without the benefit of a good sleeping bag in addition to the warmth provided by a wood-burning stove.

[pause]

Now you'll hear the recording again.

tone

[The recording is repeated.]

[pause]

That's the end of Part Two.
Now turn to Part Three.

[pause]

PART 3
You'll hear an interview with David McKinley, who recently opened 'The Adventure Centre', an adventure sports centre in Scotland. For questions 15 to 20, choose the answer (A, B, C or D) which fits best according to what you hear. You now have one minute to look at Part Three.

[pause]

tone

Interviewer: I'm interviewing David McKinley, the co-founder of 'The Adventure Centre' which has just opened here in Scotland. David – the centre sounds wonderful, housing as it does a rock-climbing wall, a gym and a health club. But tell me, how did you initially get involved?

David: Well, I was lucky enough to enjoy a flexible work structure when I worked as a television sports cameraman, which enabled me to take it forward as an idea. But actually it all started with an ambitious idea I had back in the 1990s when I had a job as an instructor in a gym. I'd take clients climbing in the morning, then they'd go into the gym in the afternoon. The idea obviously caught people's imagination because I was contacted by Geoff Taylor, an architect who'd heard about it. We joined forces and decided on a multi-adventure centre offering lots of different activities. With Geoff's help, it went from a rather community-spirited, small-scale project to a fully commercial, profit-making enterprise.

Interviewer: And you've had a mixed career to date, haven't you?

David: Well, I did a degree in film photography, and then worked on lots of wildlife documentaries, and soon got a reputation as someone who could work in difficult places doing difficult things. I'd realised early on that I wanted an adventurous life and I didn't want a conventional job. After travelling all over the world for ten years, though, I felt that working in films long term wasn't a stable option. Luckily, throughout this time, I'd also been connected with a gym which helped sports companies to develop products – out of interest really – but thanks to this, I developed a strong commercial awareness which has helped me in this current venture.

Interviewer: I'm sure … and what about you as a person – how would you sum yourself up?

David: Well, I love being active and I'm not very good at being tied to a desk! It's true that I'm not afraid to make mistakes, although I hope I don't make <u>too</u> many – it's just that I tend to rush in without thinking things through sufficiently beforehand and other people often criticise you for that. But basically, I'm an ideas person. I'm excited by ideas and I can't wait to put them into action.

Interviewer: And doubtless you've had some bad times during your career as well as good. What have been the most memorable?

David: There've been some bad moments in the business, especially at the start. So many customers were contacting me and it was hard to cope, but it was also exciting to think my name was getting known! I suppose the thing that stands out for me has been the development of the Adventure Centre – just going in each day to the site, and seeing it grow. But I can also remember many other exciting projects - like working on a documentary film on waterfalls in South America - lots of fantastic shots, but totally exhausting!

Interviewer: You're involved in an industry that's constantly changing. What challenges do you think lie ahead?

David: Well, the last few years have seen many health clubs struggling to keep members ... going to the gym can be boring and some soon give up ... but this is less of a problem these days as many people see the gym now as a way of de-stressing mentally, so have stronger motivation. The biggest issue will be saturation, I think, as everybody targets the same market. We stand out because we not only offer a wide range of activities, but we also try and educate clients about what's involved. We're honest and prepare customers fully for adventure sports, which, frankly, can be unpredictable and risky.

Interviewer: But haven't clients' needs changed? Isn't it adventure and risk which they're now increasingly seeking?

David: Yes and no! In my experience, many customers are becoming risk averse, you know, they want to be taken away from their warm, cosy environment into an adventure sports situation which is 100 per cent safe, and that just isn't possible. We have to be straight with people and recognise that being physically active is important, but anyone wanting to combine that with the excitement of adventure sports must be aware of what's involved.

Interviewer: David McKinley, many thanks.

[pause]

Now you'll hear the recording again.

tone

[The recording is repeated.]

[pause]

That's the end of Part Three.
Now turn to Part Four.

[pause]

PART 4

Part Four consists of two tasks. You'll hear five short extracts in which people are talking about taking a gap year – the time which some young people take off from their studies to gain other experience. Look at Task 1. For questions 21 to 25, choose from the list A to H what each speaker did during their gap year. Now look at Task 2. For questions 26 to 30, choose from the list A to H the benefit of having a gap year which each speaker mentions. While you listen you must complete both tasks. You now have 45 seconds to look at Part Four.

[pause]

tone

Speaker One   Even though I wasn't short of money I wanted to get some work experience before going to university, so I decided not to jet around the globe, and found a job in the nearest town instead. I had to live in because of early shifts, and only realised on about Day Two it would mean I couldn't keep up my tennis – that was a blow at first, because I was a very keen player. But I just had to get over it and carry on – just doing that taught me a lot, actually. Anyway, I was having too much fun with the rest of the staff to fret about it – I wonder if they're all still there? The worst part of the job was when guests complained, which they frequently did!

[pause]

Speaker Two   Well, I took a gap year because I thought I hadn't seen enough of the world. I considered doing an overland trek across the Sahara or sailing round the world. Then I found a remote village in Kenya where they needed my skills – they're all football-mad there – and a Nairobi businessman agreed to pay me quite a good wage. I settled in OK, although I never got the hang of the language, and that year gave me some serious thinking time. I realised I didn't want to complete my course back home, even though I'd already spent quite a lot of money and time on it. It's all good experience anyway.

[pause]

Speaker Three   The whole thing was a disaster from start to finish. I'd had a sort of feeling it might turn out badly. We didn't have the right training or equipment, and because there was no office back-up, we couldn't get news forwarded to our families. And the leader – well, I wonder how experienced he really was. He couldn't speak the porters' language at all. You could say our pioneering spirit was crushed by the time we got back to base camp! On the other hand, we did bond as a group, and I see a couple of them regularly and have done ever since that time. So perhaps it wasn't all bad.

[pause]

Speaker Four   I know some agencies will organise your gap year and sort out, say, working for a charity, but I'd much rather do what I did – just go off on the spur of the moment and see where you end up. It was absolutely brilliant, even though it took all the money I'd saved up for it – the fare and the hotels and eating in restaurants were to blame for that. At least I know I can cope on my own now and that's a new thing for me. Sadly, I haven't managed to keep up with the people I met in all those different cultures – I'm not surprised, though – that's life.

[pause]

Speaker Five   I was told to stick to the script whether it was in French, German or Spanish. People don't even ask many questions – it got quite boring after a while, because I felt there wasn't any real communication between me and them. And if it's raining, you get wet just hopping on and off the coach. I didn't have high hopes before I started, although it certainly was a good way of earning some much-needed cash, and there were some nice people at head office, but in the end I did wonder if I couldn't have found something a bit more inspiring. How often do people get a year off in their lifetime?

[pause]

Now you'll hear the recording again.

tone

[The recording is repeated.]

[pause]

That's the end of Part Four.

*There'll now be a pause of **five minutes** for you to **copy your answers onto the separate answer sheet**. Be sure to follow the numbering of all the questions. I'll remind you when there's one minute left, so that you're sure to finish in time.*

[Teacher, pause the recording here for five minutes. Remind your students when they have one minute left.]

That's the end of the test. Please stop now. Your supervisor will now collect all the question papers and answer sheets.

Test 3 Key

Paper 1   Reading (1 hour 15 minutes)

Part 1

1 C   2 B   3 C   4 D   5 A   6 D

Part 2

7 G   8 C   9 E   10 D   11 F   12 A

Part 3

13 D   14 A   15 B   16 D   17 C   18 D   19 A

Part 4

20 B   21 C/D   22 D/C   23 A   24 B   25 C   26 B   27 D   28 A   29 C
30 A   31 B   32 D   33 C   34 B

Paper 2   Writing (1 hour 30 minutes)

Task-specific Mark Schemes
The accuracy of language, including spelling and punctuation, is assessed on the general impression scale for all tasks. Criteria for assessing specific range of language and task achievement are outlined below.

Part I

The focus of Part 1 is on content, effective organisation of the input, appropriacy of the piece(s) of writing to the intended audience, and on accuracy. Some use of key words from the input is acceptable, but candidates should have reworded phrases as far as possible. The range will be defined by the task.

Question 1

Content (points covered)
The candidate's **report** must:
• describe the candidate's time at the centre
• explain difficulty/ies candidate had
• say whether candidate recommends work experience to others.

Organisation and cohesion
Clearly organised into paragraphs with appropriate linking devices.
A variety of appropriate formats is acceptable.

Range
Language of description, explanation and recommendation.
Vocabulary related to leisure activities and work.

Register/Tone
Formal to unmarked. Must be consistent.
Polite and informative tone.

Target reader
Would be informed.

Part 2

In Part 2, candidates have more scope to display their linguistic competence and there is more latitude in the interpretation of the task. The assessment focus is mainly on content, range, and style/register, with attention paid to how successfully the candidate has produced the text type required.

Question 2

Content
The candidate's **competition entry** should identify two role models – one good, one bad – and explain reason for nominations.

Organisation and cohesion
Clearly organised into paragraphs with appropriate linking devices.

Range
Language of explanation and possibly persuasion.
Vocabulary related to sport and character.

Register/Tone
May mix registers if appropriate to approach taken by candidate.

Target reader
Would be informed.

Question 3

Content
The candidate's **article** should express opinion on whether dress reflects personality and give reasons.

Organisation and cohesion
Clearly organised into paragraphs with appropriate linking devices.

Range
Language of explanation and opinion.
Vocabulary related to clothes, style and character.

Register/Tone
May mix registers if appropriate to approach taken by candidate.

Target reader
Would be informed.

Question 4

Content
The candidate's **proposal** should describe an environmental project they want to see developed and explain how it would benefit the local community.
N.B. A project could include several environmental issues.

Organisation and cohesion
Clearly organised into paragraphs with appropriate linking devices. A variety of appropriate formats is acceptable.

Range
Language of description and explanation.
Vocabulary related to environmental issues.

Register/Tone
Formal to unmarked.

Target reader
Would be informed. Must be consistent.

Question 5 (a)

Content
The candidate's **essay** should explain how Darby Shaw became involved in the case, say whether she acted foolishly and give reasons.

Organisation and cohesion
Clearly organised into paragraphs with appropriate linking devices.

Range
Language of explanation, opinion and justification.

Register/Tone
Unmarked to formal. Must be consistent.

Target reader
Would be informed.

Question 5 (b)

Content
The candidate's **article** should explain how Jim Dixon's bad luck provides humour in *Lucky Jim*, say which scene is funniest and give reasons.

Organisation and cohesion
Clearly organised into paragraphs with appropriate linking devices.

Range
Language of explanation, opinion, justification and possibly description.
Vocabulary related to humour.

Register/Tone
May mix registers if appropriate to approach taken by candidate.

Target reader
Would be informed.

Paper 3   Use of English (1 hour)

Part 1

1 B   2 C   3 B   4 D   5 C   6 C   7 A   8 B   9 A   10 C   11 D
12 B

Part 2

13 but / yet / nevertheless / (al)though   14 much   15 up   16 whose
17 with   18 his   19 is   20 when / while / if / whilst   21 for
22 their   23 By   24 against   25 only / just   26 of   27 it

Part 3

28 primary   29 minimising   30 effectively   31 willingness   32 sympathetic
33 indispensable   34 qualification   35 practical   36 competition
37 familiarity

Part 4

38 sense   39 clear   40 sank   41 side   42 show

Part 5

43 was caused | by (the) flooding   44 does not matter | (at) what OR is not a matter of |
what   45 be able to (do it) | unless   46 have (ever / possibly) predicted | (that) we would / we
were going to   47 not doing what / as | David (had) suggested   48 made up her mind / made
her mind up | not to   49 attempts / efforts | to get in touch with   50 (has) held us | up

Paper 4   Listening (approximately 40 minutes)

Part 1

1 A   2 A   3 C   4 A   5 B   6 C

Part 2

7 list   8 fishing   9 maps   10 camping   11 coal (mining)   12 bikes / bicycles
13 collecting   14 (a) runaway success

Part 3

15 B   16 D   17 C   18 B   19 D   20 A

Part 4

21 A   22 C   23 H   24 F   25 E   26 E   27 F   28 H   29 C   30 D

Transcript   *This is the Cambridge Certificate in Advanced English Listening Test. Test Three.
I'm going to give you the instructions for this test. I'll introduce each part of the test
and give you time to look at the questions.*

At the start of each piece you'll hear this sound:

tone

You'll hear each piece twice.

*Remember, while you're listening, write your answers on the **question paper**. You'll
have **five minutes** at the end of the test to **copy your answers onto the separate
answer sheet**.*

*There'll now be a pause. Please ask any questions now, because you must not speak
during the test.*

[pause]

PART 1

Now open your question paper and look at Part One.

[pause]

You'll hear three different extracts. For questions one to six, choose the answer (A, B, or C) which fits best according to what you hear. There are two questions for each extract.

Extract 1

You overhear two people talking at a party about a round-the-world trip.

Now look at questions one and two.

[pause]

tone

Woman:	You're the man who spent years travelling round the world on a motorbike!
Man:	That's right.
Woman:	What made you decide to travel in that way?
Man:	Well, taking my car seemed a bit unadventurous and anyway I really wanted to get off the beaten track and experience life in remote corners of the world.
Woman:	Did you think about cycling?
Man:	That would've been cheaper – no fuel costs to pay. And of course it would've been more ecologically friendly, but I don't think I could've handled all that pedalling up mountains!
Woman:	My son's talking about doing an admittedly much shorter trip, going across Australia on a motorbike. How should I react?
Man:	Look at it this way. I couldn't honestly say that I didn't run up against any problems or meet with hostility from time to time. But that was outweighed by the amazing reception I got 90 per cent of the time, particularly in less developed regions. It doesn't take into account either how much I learned in all sorts of ways and how that's impacted on my life. I wouldn't have missed it for anything.

[pause]

tone

[The recording is repeated.]

[pause]

Extract 2

You hear part of an interview with a sculptor.

Now look at questions three and four.

[pause]

tone

Interviewer:	You regard the racehorse and rider as your finest piece, don't you?
Man:	That's right. Strangely enough, I've always been an animal lover myself but hadn't considered such a subject until I heard the horse owner talking on television about the great affection he had for this famous horse. I was so touched by his sincerity that I decided immediately to try and capture both horse and rider in another dimension. It turned out as a tribute to the beauty of the animal and I hear the rider is amazed with the result, which I'm glad about, as it took months to complete!

Interviewer: And what would you say to any new artist today, hoping to succeed?

Man: Well, many artists today try and capture the attention of rich patrons by producing stuff they know will get them sponsorship rather than follow their own creative instincts. Some artists start by copying others and, though they can certainly learn the craft that way, ultimately it won't earn them their place in this competitive world. You must follow your heart. It's a question of confidence, too, in your own style – it's easy to doubt yourself, but it does get easier with time!

[pause]

tone

[The recording is repeated.]

[pause]

Extract 3   *You hear part of an interview with Carol Mills, who recently completed a 700-kilometre sledge race from Canada to the North Pole.*

Now look at questions five and six.

[pause]

tone

Man: Carol – congratulations on your achievement! I'm sure you learned many things on your long trip, which perhaps you can use now you're back at work…

Woman: Well, yes … it certainly was a fantastic experience. I think the main thing I'll take away from it is that if you don't look after each other's needs, you're not looking after your own! Working together was essential to our getting through the journey. I'm so used to leading a team in my job and telling others what to do, I had to change my perspective, which was hard at first.

Man: And has the experience changed the way you work, do you think?

Woman: Mmm… I've always been competitive, wanting to climb the job ladder, for example, pushing myself a lot, which is why I entered the race in the first place, I suppose. Now though, I look outwards more, at others, and if I see colleagues getting worked up about something, I always think 'there is a way around this', 'cause on the trip we just had to sort things out. We even faced a polar bear in our tent, at one point, so we had to be ready for anything!

[pause]

tone

[The recording is repeated.]

[pause]

That's the end of Part One.
Now turn to Part Two.

[pause]

PART 2

You'll hear a talk about Hugh Munro, an important figure in the history of mountain climbing in Scotland. For questions 7 to 14, complete the sentences. You now have 45 seconds to look at Part Two.

[pause]

tone

Sir Hugh Munro helped to make mountain climbing in Scotland the popular activity it is today. Hugh Munro was born in 1856. He learned to climb in the Swiss Alps, where the sport of mountaineering was just developing. Then in 1890, the Scottish Mountaineering Club, which was seeking to improve the information available for mountaineers, asked him to put together a list of all the mountains in Scotland over one thousand metres high. This is how a group of 250 Scottish mountains came to be known as 'Munros' and people today still consult his work rather than local guidebooks.

Local people had always made use of the mountain areas, but in the main they'd been exploited for cattle grazing and fishing. Gradually, however, from the nineteenth century, the infrastructure was developed and roads and railways were built right up into the remote valleys. Specialists then came and made maps of the area. So at last people could get to the Highlands more easily and find their way around.

In the early twentieth century, there was a steady increase in visitors following in Hugh Munro's footsteps. There were a number of developments in the 1930s, though, that changed things further. A new pastime which was then called hiking became popular. It was more than just country walking, more like what today we'd call backpacking because it could be combined with camping overnight, another new fashion. This meant people could visit areas of the countryside beyond the reach of public transport.

The 1930s was also the period known as The Great Depression, when a large number of industries and businesses collapsed and people were out of work. In the industrial cities of Scotland, for example, many young people who had been working in coal mining or shipbuilding had nothing to do. So they began to use the time they suddenly had on their hands to enjoy the great outdoors, and mountain climbing became a popular activity for them. Often people could not afford to take trains, so would ride bikes to reach the mountains, which could be hundreds of miles away.

Soon after Munro completed his task, people began to see it as a challenge to try to climb all his mountains. Mountaineers talk about 'collecting' them. Until 1950 only a few people, about 20 in all, had succeeded in conquering all of them. The number increased slowly until the 1980s, when climbing all the Munros suddenly became very, very popular. In the last decade, it's become what you could call a runaway success as there are now over 2,500 people who've done it, and some have completed more than one round.

[pause]

Now you'll hear the recording again.

tone

[The recording is repeated.]

[pause]

That's the end of Part Two.
Now turn to Part Three.

[pause]

PART 3   *You'll hear a radio interview with a young novelist called Nic Farren, who is talking about his writing and his experience of working in bookshops. For questions 15 to 20, choose the answer (A, B, C or D) which fits best according to what you hear. You now have one minute to look at Part Three.*

[pause]

tone

Interviewer: Today I'm talking to Nic Farren, who has recently had his first novel published. Nic, congratulations! I understand it was written while you were also studying Fine Art at university and working part-time in a local bookshop. Wasn't that hard?

Nic: Yes – quite tricky, although at least that meant I had access to source material, especially the work of other writers, which did feed into my style of writing, plus more factual material for my research for the novel. I didn't do a lot of that, though, to be honest, because the story was based almost entirely on my own experiences. But as time went on, I began to lose interest in my course and the writing quickly took over to the point where I kind of begrudged spending any time at all on coursework.

Interviewer: And what about the process of writing? Many writers carry a notebook for recording ideas. Do you?

Nic: Oh yes, the famous 'writer's notebook'! Well, of course you're always advised to do that, and some brilliant stuff in novels has probably been created in that way, because it's the sort of thing that can inspire you with new ideas when you're struggling. But as it turned out, I covered the pages of mine with more drawings than writing – I was always a bit scared that someone would see what I'd scribbled down there and think it was rubbish, so I tended not to commit much else to it.

Interviewer: So is your novel on sale in the shop where you work?

Nic: Not yet, and I haven't even told my colleagues I've written one, as there's always someone who's in the middle of writing something. If I ever have to sell it to someone… I can't imagine just putting it in the bag as usual. I don't think I'll be able to resist telling them who the author is! One colleague even had to stand by while copies of his novel were packed up and sent back to the publisher because no-one had bought them. I'm not expecting that but it'll be strange to see my book there on the shelves on its first day.

Interviewer: Now, we've talked about the bookshop where you work. Tell me, what's the attraction?

Nic:	Well, I've just always loved bookshops. Before I started I always had this image of whiling away my working hours talking to like-minded people about favourite books, in a tranquil environment, around books by writers that have changed the world. The reality, of course, turned out to be very different – no time to chat, and lots of holiday reads on the shelves! But working with books is special to me. I can't open a box of new books without dipping into one of them.
Interviewer:	And you first worked in a small second-hand bookshop. What was that like?
Nic:	Oh, a great experience. It was run by a woman called Mary. It had clearly once been quite smart but was now rather run-down. There was lots of classic literature – and, strangely, plenty of books about dogs, because a customer had apparently once asked for them. He never came back to buy them, so she didn't make that mistake again. It was pretty relaxed there – one guy even came in once and made himself some tea in the staff kitchen! But one of my customers actually said one day, 'Mary has oceans of books and she lets me browse through them as long as I please.' That summed up its appeal to customers, I think.
Interviewer:	Mmm, it's a lovely image, and quite different from the usual one of booksellers!
Nic:	Hmm, well, of course there was one very famous writer who worked in a bookshop and was very scathing about his experience! In his writing he comes across as being rather rude and grumpy. It's just on the surface, of course, but I'm afraid that negative image may well have stuck. Luckily though, lots of booksellers are perfectly pleasant, even with customers who'd try anyone's patience. They've read more books than you can possibly imagine, and will tell you in great detail about their personal favourites – you hear a lot about those ...
Interviewer:	Oh dear, but could you see bookselling as your long-term career, rather than art or writing?
Nic:	I don't think so.

[pause]

Now you'll hear the recording again.

tone

[The recording is repeated.]

[pause]

That's the end of Part Three.
Now turn to Part Four.

[pause]

PART 4

Part Four consists of two tasks. You'll hear five short extracts in which people are talking about awards they have received in recognition of achievements in their working lives. Look at Task 1. For questions 21 to 25, choose from the list A to H what each person's achievement was. Now look at Task 2. For questions 26 to 30, choose from the list A to H the result of each person's achievement. While you listen you must complete both tasks. You now have 45 seconds to look at Part Four.

[pause]

tone

Speaker One   I've always considered myself an unassuming person. I've always worked hard when I've been asked to – manning the phones, fixing the heating from time to time. But I never imagined I'd be called on to show another side – try to summon up enough coolness and presence of mind to deal with what happened. I am truly honoured to be given this award for what you have so kindly called my daring in braving the smoke and flames that night. My satisfaction, however, comes from knowing that if I hadn't done what I did, someone could have been injured, or worse. So, I am only too delighted to accept the award.

[pause]

Speaker Two   … during a period when new customers have been hard to find for most of our competitors, I can now confirm that we have nine per cent more customers overall, and so increased sales. I realise that I am being given this award because 40 per cent of the new customers who filled out the questionnaire, for some strange reason very kindly mentioned my (and I quote!) 'flash of inspiration' as one of their reasons for coming back to our stores again after a first visit. I can only say that I am delighted, although I'm sure that somebody would have come up with the idea sooner or later! Thank you for voting me the 'Worker of the Year'.

[pause]

Speaker Three   I'm really very moved to be receiving this. Over all these years in public service – and I can hardly believe it's as many as you say it is! – I've certainly witnessed some pretty stressful situations – you know what I mean – but it's … it isn't just sending people back to their homes and families when they're better, is it? That's only part of the story. No, the important thing is that people are cared for as they should be, thanks to all of you wonderful people, not just me. And that's satisfaction. That's what I'll be able to look back on, and that's the real satisfaction, and that's what keeps me going through thick and thin.

[pause]

Speaker Four   When the managing director shook my hand just now and said 'having won through against all the odds', I could hardly believe he was actually talking about me. But, to be honest, it was very hard indeed trying to cope with a full-time job, what with being busy every single evening. I realise that a certificate of this kind isn't the same as an award for, say, bravery – and it hasn't got a lot to do with me sitting at my computer keying in cash flows, or advising people what to do with their hard-earned savings. But it's certainly boosted my ego, and you never know, it might come in useful!

[pause]

Speaker Five   It seems to me there are other members of the team who are far more deserving than I am. But looking back, I can't help thinking about the changes I've overseen on the shop floor – we've gone from steam power to robots. Although not all of them have perhaps been for the better – well, some you win, some you lose! – it's very rewarding that I've been acknowledged as instrumental in bringing many of them in, not to mention trying to keep everybody happy at the same time. But what next? Well, I fully intend to be here to find out. But seriously, nobody could have inherited better people to work with. I can't thank you enough.

[pause]

Now you'll hear the recording again.

tone

[The recording is repeated.]

[pause]

That's the end of Part Four.

*There'll now be a pause of **five minutes** for you to **copy your answers onto the separate answer sheet**. Be sure to follow the numbering of all the questions. I'll remind you when there's one minute left, so that you're sure to finish in time.*

[Teacher, pause the recording here for five minutes. Remind your students when they have one minute left.]

That's the end of the test. Please stop now. Your supervisor will now collect all the question papers and answer sheets.

Test 4 Key

Paper 1   Reading (1 hour 15 minutes)

Part 1

1 B   2 D   3 C   4 C   5 C   6 B

Part 2

7 C   8 G   9 E   10 A   11 F   12 D

Part 3

13 D   14 C   15 B   16 C   17 A   18 C   19 C

Part 4

20 D   21 A   22 C   23 D   24 B   25 E   26 A   27 E   28 C   29 B
30 E   31 C   32 E   33 C/D   34 D/C

Paper 2   Writing (1 hour 30 minutes)

Task-specific Mark Schemes

The accuracy of language, including spelling and punctuation, is assessed on the general impression scale for all tasks. Criteria for assessing specific range of language and task achievement are outlined below.

Part I

The focus of Part 1 is on content, effective organisation of the input, appropriacy of the piece(s) of writing to the intended audience, and on accuracy. Some use of key words from the input is acceptable, but candidates should have reworded phrases as far as possible. The range will be defined by the task.

Question 1

Content (points covered)
The candidate's **letter** must:
• describe their experience
• say whether they would recommend the course or not
• give reasons for their opinion.

Organisation and cohesion
Clearly organised into paragraphs with appropriate linking devices.
Letter format with suitable opening and closing formulae.
Early reference to reason for writing.

Range
Language of description, recommendation and justification.
Vocabulary related to English-language courses.

Register/Tone
Informal to unmarked. Must be consistent.
Friendly informative tone.

Target reader
Would be informed.

Part 2

In Part 2, candidates have more scope to display their linguistic competence and there is more latitude in the interpretation of the task. The assessment focus is mainly on content, range, and style/register, with attention paid to how successfully the candidate has produced the text type required.

Question 2

Content
The candidate's **essay** should state opinion and give reasons.
N.B. Allow a wide interpretation of music star.

Organisation and cohesion
Clearly organised into paragraphs with appropriate linking devices.

Range
Language of opinion, comparison and evaluation.
Vocabulary related to music, entertainment and marketing.

Register/Tone
Unmarked to formal. Must be consistent.

Target reader
Would be informed.

Question 3

Content
The candidate's **article** should describe important characteristics of the best friend, say what important lessons have been learned from the friend and say if the friendship will change.

Organisation and cohesion
Clearly organised into paragraphs with appropriate linking devices.

Range
Language of description, explanation and speculation.
Vocabulary related to friendships and characteristics.

Register/Tone
May mix registers if appropriate to approach taken by candidate.

Target reader
Would be informed.

Question 4

Content
The candidate's **report** should briefly describe two TV shows or types of TV show, explain why they preferred one or the other and say whether they would consider participating in a reality show.

Organisation and cohesion
Clearly organised into paragraphs with appropriate linking devices.

Range
Language of description, explanation and opinion.
Vocabulary related to TV.

Register/Tone
Unmarked to formal. Must be consistent.

Target reader
Would be informed.

Question 5 (a)

Content
The candidate's **essay** should compare the characters of Jim Dixon and Professor Welch, say who the candidate feels more sympathetic towards and give reasons.

Organisation and cohesion
Clearly organised into paragraphs with appropriate linking devices.

Range
Language of comparison, opinion and justification.
Vocabulary related to the story.

Register/Tone
Unmarked to formal. Must be consistent.

Target reader
Would be informed.

Question 5 (b)

Content
The candidate's **article** should say which two events are the most visual and give reasons.

Organisation and cohesion
Clearly organised into paragraphs with appropriate linking devices.

Range
Language of description, opinion and justification.
Vocabulary related to the story.

Register/Tone
May mix registers if appropriate to approach taken by candidate.

Target reader
Would be informed.

Paper 3 Use of English (1 hour)

Part 1

1 C   2 D   3 B   4 A   5 C   6 B   7 D   8 C   9 A   10 B
11 D   12 D

Part 2

13 which   14 off   15 least   16 because   17 to   18 last / past
19 with / by   20 if / though   21 no   22 will   23 where   24 for
25 whose   26 Since   27 there

Part 3

28 impressive   **29** enthusiastic   **30** recognition   **31** realist   **32** outstanding
33 competitive   **34** appearances   **35** ensure   **36** maturity   **37** flawless

Part 4

38 hurt   **39** dry   **40** marked   **41** face   **42** shot

Part 5

43 took the blame / responsibility | for   **44** matter how (hard / much) | we tried / we
would try   **45** taking gloves | in case it gets   **46** was / had been warned | to stay / keep
away   **47** having been able / being able | to get / to have   **48** (that) he was meant | to
give   **49** has been | a drop in   **50** my bitter disappointment | I was not

Paper 4   Listening (approximately 40 minutes)

Part 1

1 A   2 C   3 A   4 B   5 C   6 C

Part 2

7 arena   **8** 224   **9** turning tail   **10** gate   **11** hurt   **12** (the) open   **13** ribbon
14 unpredictable

Part 3

15 C   **16** D   **17** A   **18** A   **19** B   **20** A

Part 4

21 G   **22** C   **23** E   **24** B   **25** A   **26** D   **27** C   **28** B   **29** E   **30** H

Transcript   *This is the Cambridge Certificate in Advanced English Listening Test. Test Four.*

*I'm going to give you the instructions for this test. I'll introduce each part of the test
and give you time to look at the questions.*

At the start of each piece you'll hear this sound:

tone

You'll hear each piece twice.

*Remember, while you're listening, write your answers on the **question paper**. You'll
have **five minutes** at the end of the test to **copy your answers onto the separate
answer sheet**.*

*There'll now be a pause. Please ask any questions now, because you must not speak
during the test.*

[pause]

PART 1   *Now open your question paper and look at Part One.*

                          [pause]

                          You'll hear three different extracts. For questions one to six, choose the answer (A, B, or C) which fits best according to what you hear. There are two questions for each extract.

Extract 1   *You overhear a sportsman called Alex talking to his coach.*

                          Now look at questions one and two.

                          [pause]

                          tone

        Alex: I can't seem to motivate myself any more. I know I've still got it in me to improve my fitness and my ability in sport but I can't seem to get there. What can I do?
       Coach: At least you recognise the need to get motivated, Alex. That's a good start. Any coach will tell you that being psychologically motivated is crucial to being the best in sport. Not everyone experiences the same kind of motivation and I think there are at least two main kinds. There's ego orientation – playing sport because you want to be the winner; or task orientation – continually trying to improve your own personal best performances.
        Alex: I know my problem. When I'm winning, everything's fine. I'm totally motivated. But when things aren't working out, like now, I give up too easily. So I've got to push myself. I'll have to aim as high as I possibly can and even if I fall short of my targets, hopefully I'll still achieve something. It sounds easy to say, but it's going to take hard work.

                          [pause]

                          tone

                          [The recording is repeated.]

                          [pause]

Extract 2   *You hear part of a radio programme in which a reporter called Toby Beesley is talking about a museum located in a castle.*

                          Now look at questions three and four.

                          [pause]

                          tone

   Presenter: In this city we're all very proud of our castle, but how many of us can say, hand on heart, we've been round its museum? Well, yesterday we sent our reporter Toby Beesley to the Castle Museum to see what it's like.

Toby:	At the entrance you're greeted by a notice describing it as the largest, most comprehensive city museum in the world. But many of its galleries are still very traditional with exhibits in glass cases. They quite deliberately avoid technological gadgetry in terms of CD-ROMs and holograms, etc. because, we're told, that wouldn't fit the dignity of the castle. Apparently, no one's saying that those things are in themselves undignified, but rather that they don't sit very comfortably in what's also a historical building. So this is a must for people who love the rather dusty quiet of a conventional exhibition with plenty of notices in a range of small print to peer at.
Presenter:	Thanks to Toby for that. And now here's Sophie, to tell us about the weekly farmers' market …

[pause]

tone

[The recording is repeated.]

[pause]

Extract 3 | *You hear part of an interview with Adam Harrabin, who uses a metal detector, a hand-held machine which can discover metal buried in the ground.*

Now look at questions five and six.

[pause]

tone

Presenter:	So, Adam, can you tell us a bit about your metal detecting?
Adam:	Well, of course, the metal detector only does the easy bit, then I have to pick my spade up and get down to work! So far I've retrieved a couple of watches and a gold ring – hard to say how much they're worth. But my main find has been this ancient Roman coin, and what's important about it is that it was found on a beach where historians didn't think the Romans had ever been. So if people complain about all these holes in the sand, well, we're rewriting history.
Presenter:	Using a metal detector's quite popular now, isn't it?
Adam:	Yes, it is. In theory you could go all over the country with a metal detector, but I find it easier, transport-wise, staying close to home. I never let on to anybody exactly where I'm searching, though – that's the fun of it for me, really – looking for clues that only I know about. And people find it exciting, of course – you can turn up really quite valuable things that someone might have dropped yesterday or a thousand years ago.

[pause]

tone

[The recording is repeated.]

[pause]

That's the end of Part One.
Now turn to Part Two.

[pause]

PART 2   *You'll hear part of a programme in which an Australian sheep farmer called Keith*
                          Reid is talking about a local event known as the Morongla Sheepdog Trials. For
                          questions 7 to 14, complete the sentences. You now have 45 seconds to look at Part
                          Two.

                          [pause]

                          tone

Interviewer: How many of us see dogs as working animals? But there's one dog – a
                sheepdog – that really does work hard for a living, controlling herds of sheep
                in absolute co-operation with a farmer. In Australia, as far back as the 1870s,
                the skill of these working dogs has been tested in competitions, known as
                trials. I joined Keith Reid, a sheep farmer in the small farming community of
                Morongla, for a very special occasion.

Keith: We host a country show here every year, but we needed to raise money
                to modernise the arena we use for the show, so in August we held our
                first-ever Sheepdog Trials. I'm very pleased it turned out as well as it did.
                About four hundred sheepdogs regularly take part in trials all over Australia
                and we got two hundred and twenty-four dogs. Not a bad turnout for our first
                event. We didn't expect more than a hundred and seventy-five.

                The basics of trialling haven't changed much over the years. Each team –
                that's the sheepdog handler, the dog and three sheep – has fifteen minutes
                to complete the course. The team starts with a hundred points and moves
                around the course, losing points for various offences. For instance, points are
                lost if the dog moves its head away from the sheep at any time – we call this
                'turning tail'. There are two offences that result in automatic disqualification.
                The first is when the dog bites a sheep. Fortunately, that doesn't happen
                often. The second is known as 'crossing', which is when the dog passes
                between the sheep and the handler. The aim of the whole thing is to bring the
                sheep to you, not drive them away!

                Our course begins with three sheep at one end of the field and the dog
                and handler at the other. The trial concludes when the sheep have entered
                the enclosure and the handler has secured the gate. The dog must bring the
                sheep to the handler in a straight line; we call this stage 'the draw'. Once
                they set off they can only stop at fixed points – generally near the obstacles.
                There's only one situation where the handler can ask for a rerun – and that's if
                a sheep is hurt during the competition.

                We've got four levels in our trials: beginning with what's called 'encourage',
                then we have 'novice', then 'improver' and finally the top one which goes by
                the name of 'open'. Once a dog wins at one level, it moves up to the next.
                The whole event lasts for three days and then the top three dogs will get a
                ribbon and a twenty-kilo bag of dog biscuits for their efforts! And the handlers
                walk off with a trophy.

                It all sounds easy, but believe me, it isn't. The great levellers in any
                sheepdog trial are the sheep. They can be incredibly stubborn and
                unpredictable, but anyone who thinks sheep are silly has got a lot to
                learn.

                [pause]

                Now you'll hear the recording again.

tone

[The recording is repeated.]

[pause]

That's the end of Part Two.
Now turn to Part Three.

[pause]

PART 3   *You'll hear part of an interview with an actor called Peter Jameson, who is talking about his career. For questions 15 to 20, choose the answer (A, B, C or D) which fits best according to what you hear.*

You now have one minute to look at Part Three.

[pause]

tone

Interviewer: In the studio with me tonight is the famous actor, Peter Jameson, who is known above all for his classical roles on stage, particularly in Shakespeare plays. Peter, was it your choice to appear so often in this type of play or the prejudice of casting directors?

Peter: That's an interesting question. Let me answer by giving you an example. Years ago, I wanted to play a rather unusual detective in a series on a new TV channel, and when my agent put my name up for it they said 'No, no, no, he's too posh for commercial television.' At which my agent hit the roof, quite rightly so. I've always seen myself as an actor, a jobbing actor doing whatever comes along, rather than exclusively classical roles, Shakespeare and so on, although of course I do find those fascinating.

Interviewer: And your voice is, perhaps to your irritation, what people often pick up on because its range is unusual … and its quality. Were you born with it or did you develop it over time?

Peter: Um. It was I suppose a gift originally, but I've had coaching – several people here in the UK. And then when I went to America on tour, microphones were barred in the Gershwin Theatre. And I then said, 'Look, I can't get through this. You've got to get me a voice coach.' And he came three days a week and he allied voice production with the Alexander Relaxation Technique, and he, more than anybody I think, put a kind of microphone in my throat so that I could … even when I had a cold, I could speak above it.

Interviewer: In your recent role of Prospero in the play *The Tempest,* it seemed to me that you brought out the darker edges of your voice sometimes. You also brought out his anger particularly. This is slightly against type for you, isn't it?

Peter: It's something that's dogged me throughout my career. I do have a reputation for being rather gentle and likeable – a totally unearned reputation, I have to say. But that's I suppose what comes across to the audience. That's why I relish the chance to play more demanding and complex roles like Prospero.

Interviewer: I remember seeing you playing four big parts in close succession, and I don't generally ask actors but, about um … line learning, because it's part of the trade, but it did astonish me that you must've had thousands of lines in your head at that point.

Peter: I don't know whether I could do it so easily now, twenty years on, but I've always been blessed with a sort of photographic memory, right from my earliest childhood. My subject at university was history actually, for which a memory is essential. Um … and as the years have gone by, the photographs have got a bit blurred round the edges, but they're still visible, I think.

Interviewer: Most of your theatre performances have vanished – only a few, sadly, have been recorded on tape but TV does of course survive. Have you watched your most famous series on TV – *The Romans*?

Peter: When it first went out, we were still filming episode seven, out of thirteen episodes, and episode one started going out on air. So it wouldn't have been a good idea to watch it then. I've always loathed watching myself anyway, but then about ten years later I was … some friends kind of locked me into a house in California and over the weekend, made me see the whole thing. Since then I check into hotels all over the world and switch the telly on and … they're showing reruns of it. There's no escape.

Interviewer: And when you finally got to watch *The Romans*, you were impressed by it, presumably?

Peter: I was and the great thing about it was the script. It was funny and it was violent. In a curious way it was totally contemporary – while being set in ancient Rome, which is what at the end of the book it purports to be, when my character says, 'I'll speak to you in all those years hence, I'll speak to you in a language you'll understand.' And the writer got that absolutely right.

Interviewer: And those kind of television parts don't come along very often.

[pause]

Now you'll hear the recording again.

tone

[The recording is repeated.]

[pause]

That's the end of Part Three.
Now turn to Part Four.

[pause]

PART 4   *Part Four consists of two tasks. You'll hear five short extracts in which students on art courses are talking about their experiences. Look at Task 1. For questions 21 to 25, choose from the list A to H the difficulties each speaker has had to overcome. Now look at Task 2. For questions 26 to 30, choose from the list A to H what each speaker enjoys most about the process of creating art. While you listen you must complete both tasks. You now have 45 seconds to look at Part Four.*

[pause]

tone

Speaker One   I find the lifestyle of a big city very stimulating. It's multicultural, full of activity – but I'd be the first to admit that there are frustrations, for me as an artist, living there. Unfortunately the grey surroundings affect the way my work ends up looking, particularly the colour scheme, so I've had to concentrate my efforts on counteracting that. I tend to shy away from imagining the outcome to a piece of work. Instead I'll sit alone in my bedroom, which is a vast loft space and so doubles as a workroom, scribbling notes on a scrap of paper. That's the real buzz for me.

[pause]

Speaker Two   After several years spent working, I've returned to art school full-time. There are no funds available for students taking a second degree, so it's hard to come up with the rent for my tiny flat but I just about manage it. But luckily my mother's converted part of her house into an art studio, so that helps. As an artist I'm fascinated by the human form. My paintings are self-portraits, so before I start painting I can literally spend hours making observational studies of myself. Sometimes I get so absorbed, the final piece never happens! I also use family photos as the work develops, working in colours similar to artists like Modigliani and Matisse.

[pause]

Speaker Three   I picked up pen and paper at an early age – I used to draw characters from my favourite books. But at college I have to show I can handle different media, so I spend hours there grappling with painting, to keep up with the other students, who are very competitive, and I think I hold my own. When I'm alone, though, I'll always return to pen and ink. Strangely, once I've found a subject, I actually get a lot out of just going to written accounts of what other artists have done – it sparks off original ideas of my own. I'd like to have a career illustrating children's books one day, although I don't imagine I'll make much money from it.

[pause]

Speaker Four   I work as a part-time landscape architect in the city, only part-time but it provides money and free time for my art studies, which I work on for the rest of the week. I live in a cottage, and my studio is actually the main room, so it's tricky when anyone comes round, so I have to be very well organised. I like experimenting with different media, but what truly gets the creativity flowing is being out taking shots of the countryside, whatever the weather, and then printing them off on my computer. They can develop into anything, even townscapes or portraits, but somehow they'll always echo my passion for the landscape.

[pause]

Speaker Five   My response to art and other artists' work used to be a matter of writing copious notes – but that got me nowhere. My own work really took off when I discovered oil paints. For me there's nothing that compares with dabbling with a rainbow of paints and seeing what comes. And achieving the right combination can evoke so much emotion in the viewer. I've got three young sons to bring up, which could take time away from my art, so I have to make sure I've got adequate childcare arrangements in place. But I've got a scholarship to study in Los Angeles soon, so we're all moving there, although they're not keen on big cities.

[pause]

Now you'll hear the recording again.

tone

[The recording is repeated.]

[pause]

That's the end of Part Four.

There'll now be a pause of **five minutes** *for you to* **copy your answers onto the separate answer sheet***. Be sure to follow the numbering of all the questions. I'll remind you when there's one minute left, so that you're sure to finish in time.*

[Teacher, pause the recording here for five minutes. Remind your students when they have one minute left.]

That's the end of the test. Please stop now. Your supervisor will now collect all the question papers and answer sheets.

UNIVERSITY *of* CAMBRIDGE
ESOL Examinations

S A M P L E

Candidate Name
If not already printed, write name
in CAPITALS and complete the
Candidate No. grid (in pencil)

Candidate Signature ....

Examination Title

Centre

Supervisor:
If the candidate is ABSENT or has WITHDRAWN shade here ▭

Centre No.

Candidate No.

Examination Details

0	0	0	0
1	1	1	1
2	2	2	2
3	3	3	3
4	4	4	4
5	5	5	5
6	6	6	6
7	7	7	7
8	8	8	8
9	9	9	9

Candidate Answer Sheet

Instructions

Use a PENCIL (B or HB).

Mark ONE letter for each question.

For example, if you think B is the right answer to the question, mark your answer sheet like this:

0 A B ▬ D E F G H

Rub out any answer you wish to change using an eraser.

1	A B C D E F G H
2	A B C D E F G H
3	A B C D E F G H
4	A B C D E F G H
5	A B C D E F G H
6	A B C D E F G H
7	A B C D E F G H
8	A B C D E F G H
9	A B C D E F G H
10	A B C D E F G H
11	A B C D E F G H
12	A B C D E F G H
13	A B C D E F G H
14	A B C D E F G H
15	A B C D E F G H
16	A B C D E F G H
17	A B C D E F G H
18	A B C D E F G H
19	A B C D E F G H
20	A B C D E F G H

21	A B C D E F G H
22	A B C D E F G H
23	A B C D E F G H
24	A B C D E F G H
25	A B C D E F G H
26	A B C D E F G H
27	A B C D E F G H
28	A B C D E F G H
29	A B C D E F G H
30	A B C D E F G H
31	A B C D E F G H
32	A B C D E F G H
33	A B C D E F G H
34	A B C D E F G H
35	A B C D E F G H
36	A B C D E F G H
37	A B C D E F G H
38	A B C D E F G H
39	A B C D E F G H
40	A B C D E F G H

Sample answer sheet: Paper 3

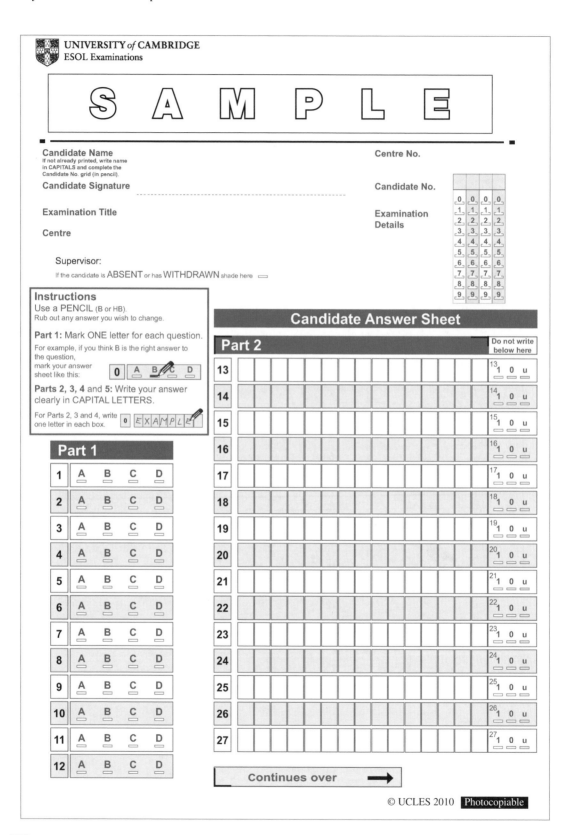

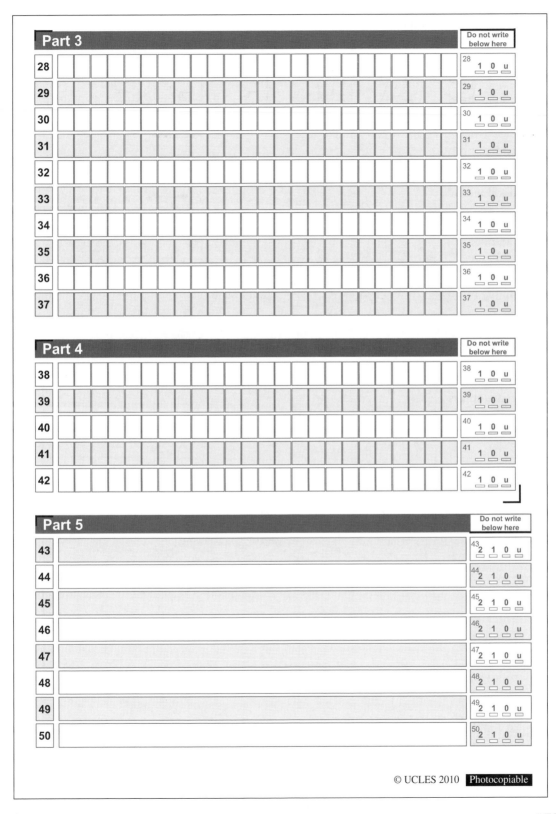

UNIVERSITY *of* **CAMBRIDGE**
ESOL Examinations

Candidate Name
If not already printed, write name
in CAPITALS and complete the
Candidate No. grid (in pencil).

Candidate Signature

Examination Title

Centre

Supervisor:
If the candidate is ABSENT or has WITHDRAWN shade here ▭

Test version: A B C D E F J K L M N   Special arrangements: S H

Centre No.

Candidate No.

**Examination
Details**

Candidate Answer Sheet

Instructions

Use a PENCIL (B or HB).
Rub out any answer you wish to change using an eraser.

Parts 1, 3 and **4:**
Mark ONE letter for each question.

For example, if you think **B** is the
right answer to the question, mark
your answer sheet like this:

Part 2:
Write your answer clearly in CAPITAL LETTERS.

Write one letter or number in each box.
If the answer has more than one word, leave one
box empty between words.

For example:

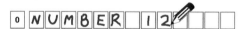

Turn this sheet over to start.

Part 1

	A	B	C
1	⎵	⎵	⎵
2	⎵	⎵	⎵
3	⎵	⎵	⎵
4	⎵	⎵	⎵
5	⎵	⎵	⎵
6	⎵	⎵	⎵

Part 2 (Remember to write in CAPITAL LETTERS or numbers)

Do not write below here

		1 0 u
7		7
8		8
9		9
10		10
11		11
12		12
13		13
14		14

Part 3

	A	B	C	D
15	⎵	⎵	⎵	⎵
16	⎵	⎵	⎵	⎵
17	⎵	⎵	⎵	⎵
18	⎵	⎵	⎵	⎵
19	⎵	⎵	⎵	⎵
20	⎵	⎵	⎵	⎵

Part 4

	A	B	C	D	E	F	G	H
21	⎵	⎵	⎵	⎵	⎵	⎵	⎵	⎵
22	⎵	⎵	⎵	⎵	⎵	⎵	⎵	⎵
23	⎵	⎵	⎵	⎵	⎵	⎵	⎵	⎵
24	⎵	⎵	⎵	⎵	⎵	⎵	⎵	⎵
25	⎵	⎵	⎵	⎵	⎵	⎵	⎵	⎵
26	⎵	⎵	⎵	⎵	⎵	⎵	⎵	⎵
27	⎵	⎵	⎵	⎵	⎵	⎵	⎵	⎵
28	⎵	⎵	⎵	⎵	⎵	⎵	⎵	⎵
29	⎵	⎵	⎵	⎵	⎵	⎵	⎵	⎵
30	⎵	⎵	⎵	⎵	⎵	⎵	⎵	⎵

Thanks and acknowledgements

The authors and publishers acknowledge the following sources of copyright material and are grateful for the permissions granted. While every effort has been made, it has not always been possible to identify the sources of all the material used, or to trace all copyright holders. If any omissions are brought to our notice, we will be happy to include the appropriate acknowledgements on reprinting.

Little, Brown Book Group Limited and Curtis Brown Group Ltd for the adapted text on p. 8 'Mrs Mintar' from *Dead and Gone* by Dorothy Simpson. Copyright © Dorothy Simpson 1999; Condé Nast Publications Limited for the adapted text on pp. 10–11 'The Modern Adventurer' from 'Trivial Pursuits' by Ed Douglas, *Condé Nast Traveller*. Copyright © The Condé Nast Publications Ltd; Adapted article on p. 12 'Bridges' by Sophia Collins. *Focus Magazine*, December 1999; Guardian News & Media Ltd for the adapted text on p. 15 'A Band and its website' from 'The Band with more hits in site' by Owen Gibson, *The Guardian* 14.2.05, and for the text on p. 60 'mrparticular.com' from 'Best of the net' by Sean Dodson, *The Guardian* 10.3.07. Copyright © Guardian News & Media Ltd 2005, 2007; NI Syndication for the adapted text on p. 18 'Rowling's promise to save forests' from 'Recycled Harry Potter to save muggle forests' by Jack Malvern, *The Times* 3.10.03 and for the adapted text on p. 90 'The Sound of Music' from ' Settling some scores' by Geoff Brown, *The Times* 30.10.01. Copyright © Times 2001, 2003 and NI Syndication.com; Penguin Books and United Agents Ltd on behalf of the author for the adapted text on p. 33 'The interview' from *A Long Way Down* by Nick Hornby. Penguin Books, 2005. Copyright © Nick Hornby 2005; New Scientist for the adapted text on pp. 36–37 from 'Calls from the Deep' by David Wolman, *New Scientist* 15 June 2002 and for the adapted text on p. 64 'Recreating sails used on Viking ships' from 'The sheep that launched 1000 ships' by Nancy Bazilchuk, *New Scientist* 24 July 2004. Copyright © New Scientist Magazine; The Independent for the adapted text on p. 38 'Thor Heyerdahl' from 'Something Wild' by Martin Buckley, *The Independent* 12.3.00. Copyright © Independent Newspapers 2000; Rambler's Association Services Ltd for the text on p. 61 'Walking the World' from *A Good Pair of Legs* by Christopher Portway. Copyright © Rambler's Association Services Ltd; Geographical Magazine for the adapted text on p. 85 'Camping in the Wild' from 'Getting away from them all' by Paul Deegan. *Geographical Magazine*, March 2007. Reproduced by permission; Pan Macmillan for the text on p. 86 'The big storm' from *The Sea* by John Banville. Picador 2005; *BBC Wildlife Magazine* for the adapted text on pp. 88–89 'Elephant Intelligence' from 'Not so Dumbo' by Claire Bruden, BBC Wildlife Magazine August 2003. Reproduced with permission; Curtis Brown for the adapted text on p. 93 'Keeping a Journal' Reproduced with permission of Curtis Brown Group Ltd, on behalf of *The Book of Life* © William Boyd 2003.

Photo Acknowledgements

The authors and publishers acknowledge the following sources of copyright material and are grateful for the permissions granted. While every effort has been made, it has not always been possible to identify the sources of all the material used, or to trace all copyright holders. If any omissions are brought to our notice, we will be happy to include the appropriate acknowledgements on reprinting.

p. 11: © Galen Rowell/Corbis; p. 37: Shutterstock/Antti Karppinen; p. 62: Columbia/Marvel / The Kobal Collection; p. 89: Shutterstock/Graeme Shannon; p. C1 (photographer): Adrianko / Alamy; p. C1 (gorilla): Biosphoto / Klein J.-L. & Hubert M.-L./BiosPhoto/Still Pictures; p. C1 (board room): Thierry Orban/Corbis Sygma; p. C2 (rowers): Sports Illustrated/Getty Images; p. C2 (children): Blend Images / Alamy; p. C2 (businessman): iStock / Barbara Reddoch; p. C3 (lecture hall): Keith Morris / Alamy; p. C3 (pandas): Sinopix/ Rex Features; p. C3 (European Parliament): Etienne Ansotte/Rex Features; p. C3 (hotels): Getty Images; p. C3 (laboratory): Getty Images/Michael Hitoshi; p. C3 (wind farm): Shutterstock/Brian A. Jackson; p. C4 (postcard): Getty Images/Gallo Images; p. C4 (presentation): Image Source / Alamy; p. C4 (mountaineer): moodboard/Corbis; p. C5 (messy office): Getty Images/Jeff Titcomb; p. C5 (woman and baby): Nonstock/ Photolibrary Group; p. C5 (Trevor Bayliss): Neville Elder/Corbis Sygma; p. C6 (maths class): Ariel Skelley/ Corbis; p. C6 (ski school): Chris McLennan / Alamy; p. C6 (birthday): Getty Images/Denis Felix; p. C6 (rock pool): thislife pictures / Alamy; p. C6 (rollercoaster): Purestock/Photolibrary Group; p. C6 (Stonehenge): Justin Kase zsixz / Alamy; p. C7 (surfer): Rick Doyle/Corbis; p. C7 (diver): Wolfgang Poelzer/Photolibrary Group; p. C7 (submersible): Jeff Rotman / Alamy; p. C8 (DJ): imagebroker / Alamy; p. C8 (musicians): Kit Kittle/Corbis; p. C8 (orchestra): Chris Fredriksson / Alamy; p. C9 (red carpet): moodboard / Alamy; p. C9 (astronauts): National Geographic/Getty Images; p. C9 (doctor): Shutterstock/Monkey Business Images; p. C9 (chefs): Shutterstock/Tonis Valing; p. C9 (designer): Getty Images/Tetra Images; p. C9 (teacher): iStock/ © Chris Schmidt; p. C10 (people chatting): Kuttig - Travel / Alamy; p. C10 (builders): Frank Chmura / Alamy; p. C10 (mother and son): CandyBox Photography / Alamy; p. C11 (grandmother and granddaughter): Getty Images/Maria Spann; p. C11 (two boys): OJO Images Ltd / Alamy; p. C11 (coffee tasters): National Geographic/Getty Images; p. C12 (Graff, iPod, Friskies, Mazda and Sony adverts): Image courtesy of The Advertising Archives; p. C12 (child with toy): Shutterstock/Anatoliy Samara; p. C12 (woman eating a chocolate): Shutterstock/Elena Kharichkina.

Picture research by Diane Jones

Design concept by Peter Ducker

Cover design by David Lawton

The recordings which accompany this book were made at dsound, London.